THE AFRICAN CALIPHS

THE AFRICAN CALIPHS

Political Leadership, Power, and
Religion in West Africa during its
Classical Islamic Age: 11th-19th Centuries

BY: DR. A. HANNIBAL HAMDALLAHI

Copyright © 2025 by Dr. A. Hannibal Hamdallahi

All rights reserved. No part of this publication may be reproduced, distributed, or transmitted in any form or by any means, including photocopying, recording, or other electronic or mechanical methods, without the prior written permission of the publisher, except in the case of brief quotations embodied in critical reviews and certain other noncommercial uses permitted by copyright law.

For Jeh

Since you left, I haven't been the same. May Allah grant you the highest level of Jannah. I look forward to the day I meet God and reunite with you, my dear Brother.

CONTENTS

Acknowledgments — viii
Illustrations — ix
Preface — xv

Introduction — 1
The Caliphate in Islamic West Africa — 13
Theory of Personalist Rule in Islamic West Africa — 27
Acquiring Caliphal Power — 37
Maintaining Caliphal Power — 67
Losing Caliphal Power — 97

Conclusion — 117
Appendix — 123
Afterwards — 139

ACKNOWLEDGMENTS

The literature presents a significant gap regarding the political leadership of West African Muslim rulers, known as African Caliphs, between the 11th and 19th centuries. Existing scholarship often focuses on specific regions, rulers, or historical episodes, neglecting a broader understanding of Islamic political leadership in West Africa. Accordingly, this study critically examines the personal skills and strategies required by African Caliphs to acquire, maintain, and sometimes lose political power while exploring the complex relationship between religion and governance during this period. The study employs a comprehensive, interdisciplinary approach, drawing from a wide array of scholarly traditions to analyze the political behavior and leadership of these rulers across time and space. The findings reveal how these leaders navigated the intersection of religion and politics and provide valuable insights into how their leadership strategies can inform contemporary political practices, particularly within African and African diasporic contexts. This research contributes to the broader field of political leadership studies and offers lessons for modern leaders, especially those of African descent, in understanding the intricate ties between religion, politics, and governance.

ILLUSTRATIONS

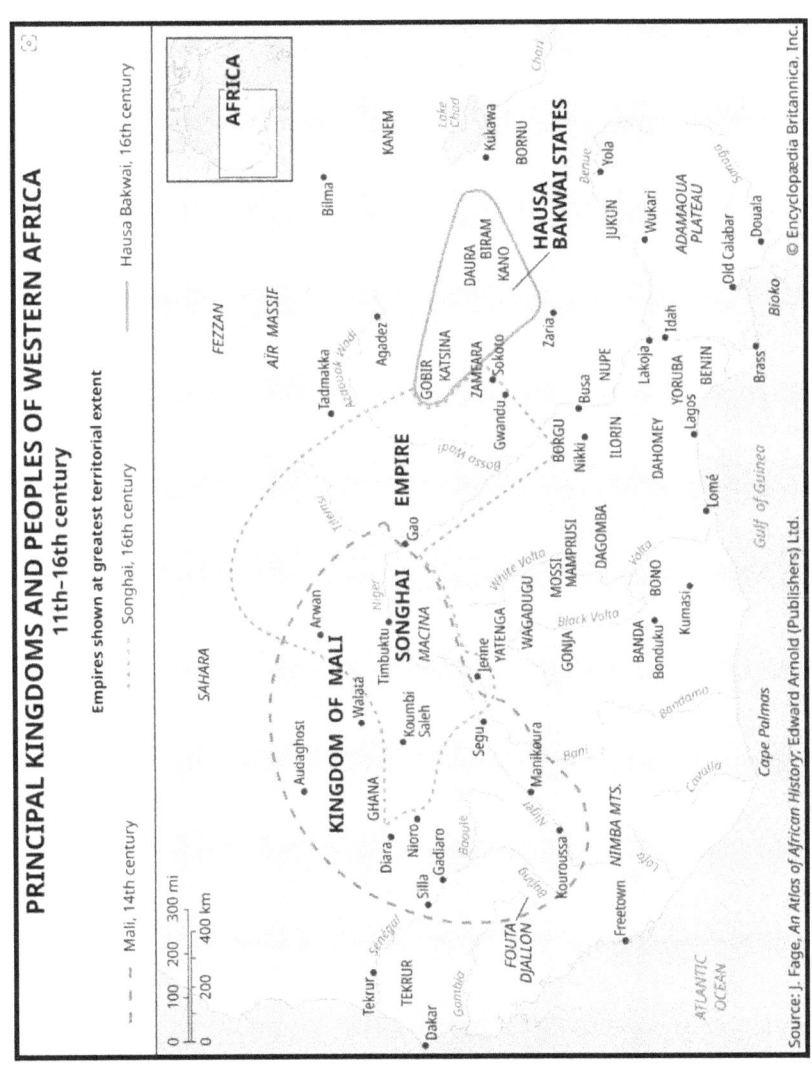

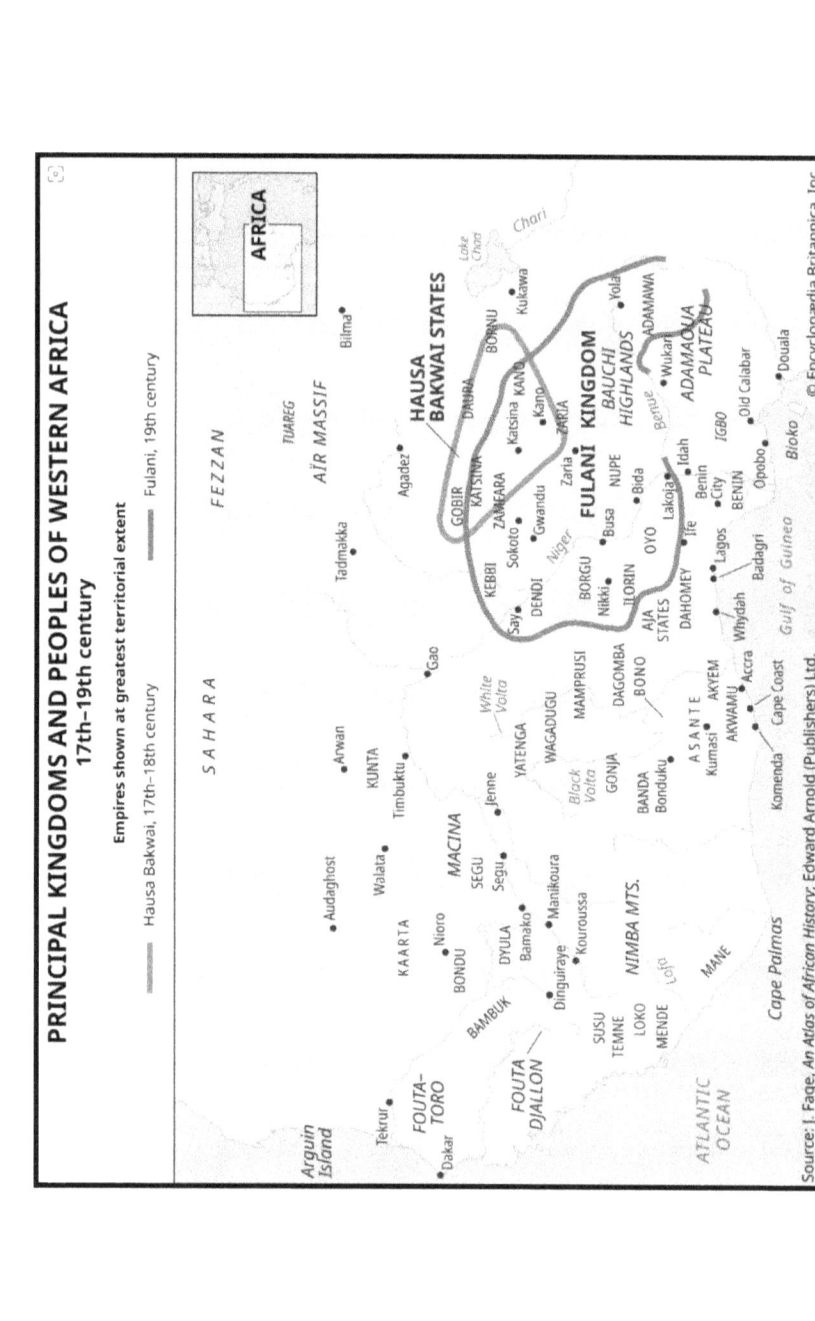

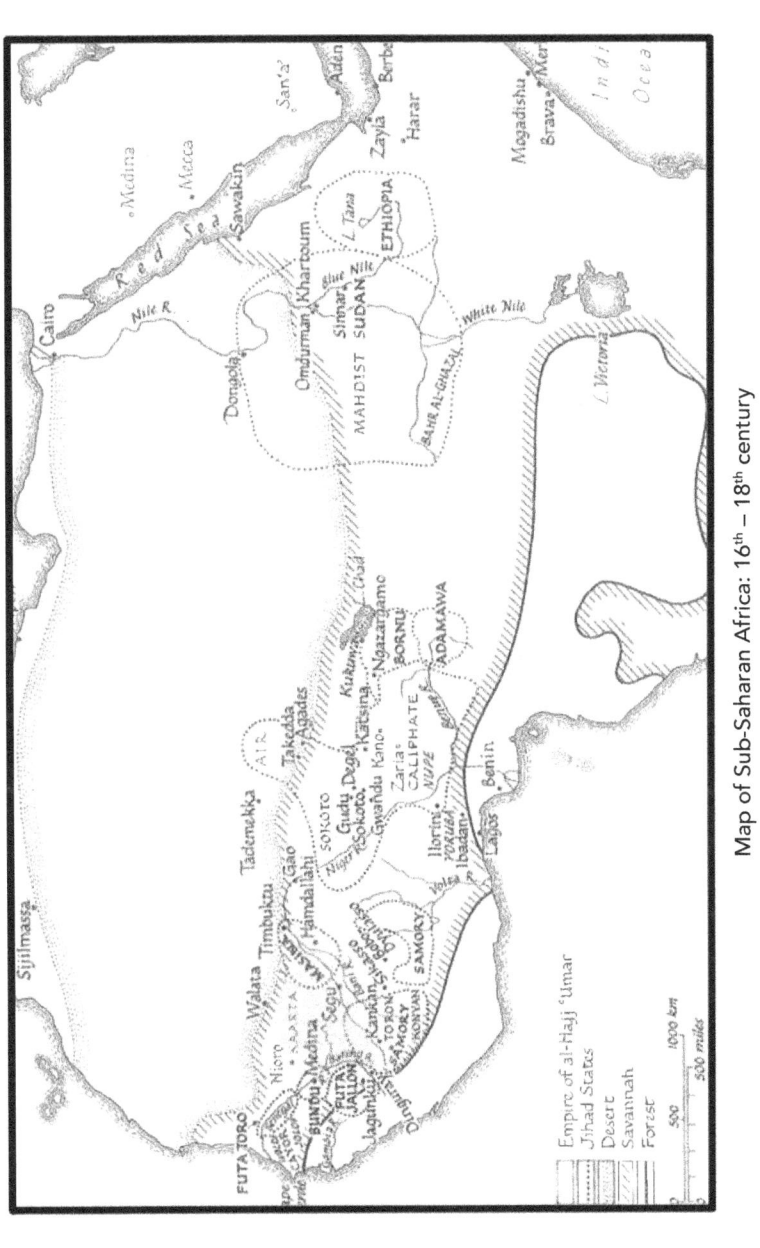

Map of Sub-Saharan Africa: 16th – 18th century

Lapidus, I. (1998). *A History of Islamic Societies.* Cambridge University Press, p. 498

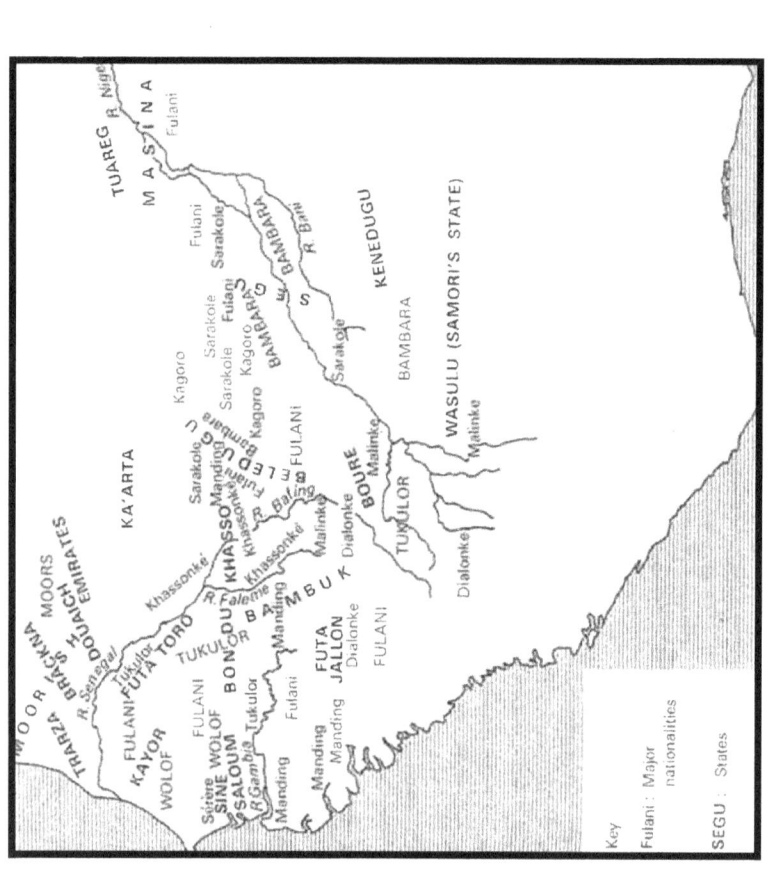

Map of states and major nationalities in mid-19th-century Western Sudan

Oloruntimehin, B.O. (1972). *The Segu Tukulor Empire*. Humanities Press, p. 5

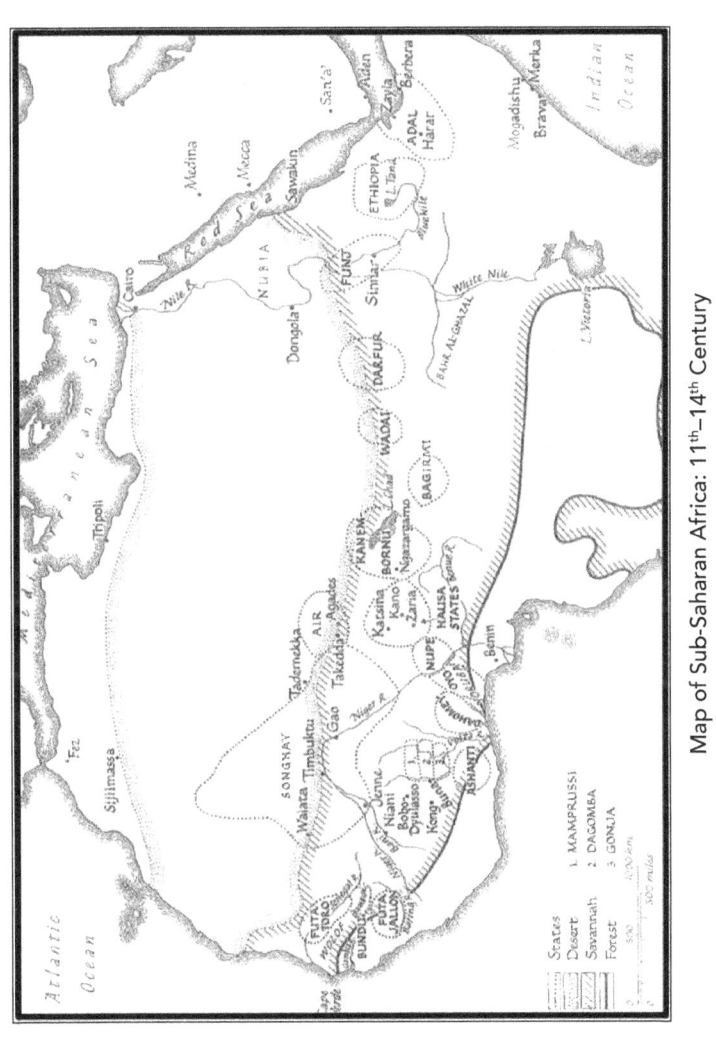

Map of Sub-Saharan Africa: 11th–14th Century

Lapidus, I. (1998). *A History of Islamic Societies*. Cambridge University Press, p. 492

PREFACE

I teach at a predominantly African American university, commonly referred to as a Historically Black College or University (HBCU). Each academic year, I teach courses on both Modern and Classical Political Theory. When I first taught these courses, my initial plan was to follow the standard canon of the discipline, covering the Greeks, the Romans, the Reformation, the Enlightenment, and so on. However, this plan was disrupted from the outset. During the customary reading of the syllabus in my first semester, several of my sophomore students politely inquired when they would study African Classics. While my syllabus included a reading of *The Egyptian Philosophers* by Molefi Kete Asante (2000), which the students appreciated, they expressed a desire for more comprehensive material. The students' questions were legitimate, and I resolved to address their request. I began searching for texts on African political thought to incorporate into the coursework, but I found few that were suitable for freshman and sophomore-level classes. One notable exception was Guy Martin's (2012) *African Political Thought*; however, this work was limited in its examination of observed political behavior. My students sought something akin to Thucydides' (2009) in-depth analysis of the political challenges faced by Pericles, Cicero's (1998) critical exploration of the political decision-making of Scipio Africanus and Hannibal Barca, or the detailed examinations of significant Roman and Greek figures, such as those found in Plutarch's (2001) *Parallel Lives*. Thus, I wrote this book for those interested in understanding the political behavior of important African leaders and the lessons their actions can offer for contemporary political discourse.

REFERENCES

Asante, M. K. (2000). *The Egyptian philosophers: Ancient African voices from Imhotep to Akhenaten*. Menaibuc.
Cicero, M. T. (1998). *On the republic* (C. W. Keyes, Trans.). Harvard University Press.
Martin, G. (2012). *African political thought*. Palgrave Macmillan.
Plutarch. (2001). *Parallel lives* (B. Perrin, Trans.). Modern Library.
Thucydides. (2009). *The histories* (M. Hammond, Trans.). Oxford University Press.

CHAPTER 1

INTRODUCTION

Shehu Usman dan Fodio, Sultan of the Sokoto Caliphate

CHAPTER 1

INTRODUCTION

This book explores the politics and pursuit of ultimate political power among precolonial West African Muslim rulers from the 11th to the 19th centuries. Its primary objective is to examine the personal skills and strategies necessary for acquiring, maintaining, and preventing the loss of ultimate political power. In this context, power refers to the exercise of authority as the official head of state, such as a kingdom, empire, or imamate. These Islamic rulers are referred to as African caliphs, a term that will be discussed further in the next chapter.

This study is valuable because it highlights a period of West African history that is often overlooked. While the history of precolonial West Africa is rightfully sensationalized due to the Transatlantic Slave Trade, the political behavior of African Muslim leaders has largely been neglected in academic circles, especially those focusing on political behavior, leadership, and administration. Despite the extensive study of African Americans in the academy, the political legacy of their ancestors, particularly precolonial West African Muslim rulers, remains largely underexplored. African Muslims formed the largest group taken from Africa to the Americas during the Transatlantic Slave Trade. Some scholars estimate that Muslims represented 40-50% of all Africans transported during this period. Outside of a small group of Africanist specialists, few scholars recognize the significance of the shared political legacy between Africans in the Diaspora and Muslims on the continent. This work seeks to fill this gap.

Another aim of this study is to examine the activities of some of the most influential political actors in West Africa between the 11th and 19th centuries. These Caliphs shaped the political, social, and religious landscape in ways that had both immediate and lasting consequences. This study focuses on the individual actions of these rulers, analyzing how they responded to the significant changes occurring over centuries, such as the rise of Islam, trade, industry, commerce, shifts in lifestyles, international relations, and universal ideas. In some regions, Islam became not only the dominant religion but also the central mode of life. Thus, this work also investigates the relationship between religion and politics. As many Africanist historians have observed, religion and politics were often intertwined in the lives of West Africa's Muslim rulers. In precolonial West Africa, the separation of church and state (or mosque and state) did not exist; in many cases, the state's existence was directly tied to the service of religion.

The interdisciplinary nature of this study draws on diverse academic fields, including political science, history, anthropology, economics, African American Studies, and African studies. By integrating these disciplines, the study offers an alternative perspective on political power, one that is rarely explored within academic circles. This work also examines the struggle of a rising faith tradition, albeit a powerful one, within African societies to advance politically. While certain research limitations (to be discussed in future chapters) may constrain the data, I aim to compensate by presenting well-documented accounts of political actions taken by African caliphs. The time frame of this study is significant, covering one of the most important eras in African history: the period of the African caliphs, which I term West Africa's Classical Islamic period. This era spans the 11th to 19th centuries, during which West Africa was home to a significant number of Muslim rulers.

This type of scholarly inquiry is not without precedent. To justify the need for the Constitution, Hamilton, Jay, and Madison wrote the Federalist Papers (Hamilton et al., 2005), examining political leadership in classical Greece and Rome. Similarly, Machiavelli (2003) crafted *The Prince*, analyzing political power through the lens of important figures throughout the history of the Italian city-states, as well as classical Greek and Roman nobility. Christine de Pizan, in her works, highlighted the lives of influential women from Biblical and classical Greece/Rome to chart new political and social paths for women (de Pizan, 1982|1405). Several centuries later, Ralph Waldo Emerson wrote *Representative Men* (1890), examining common traits among great figures throughout history, such as Plato and Goethe, and the creative genius of individuals in both thought and action. In studying African Muslim rulers, I seek to better appreciate political power through the experiences of those who preceded me.

This study differs from the aforementioned works because it exclusively examines leaders at the highest levels of government. Specifically, it focuses on their reigns, analyzing their actions to glean insights into decisions that led to either their success or downfall. A similar effort to highlight great historical figures in Africa is found in Dr. Carter G. Woodson's (1939|2016) *African Heroes and Heroines*, which aims to inform and inspire by showcasing Africa's greatest figures. While Woodson's work surveys various historical figures across a broad spectrum, my analysis is confined to West African Muslim rulers. This focus is particularly relevant as most African-descended people in the Western hemisphere trace their ancestry to West Africa. Additionally, whereas Woodson's work covers leadership in diverse capacities, my study focuses solely on the reign of African Islamic leaders.

To date, no other work offers such a comprehensive cross-sectional and analytical approach to African Islamic and political leadership within the disciplines of Political Science and African American Studies. This distinction also applies to related fields, such as African Studies and History. Most studies on African Islamic political leadership are limited to individual kingdoms/countries (Adeleye, 1977; Brenner, 1973; Klein, 1968; Charles, 1977; Rodney, 1970; Gomez, 1992; Smith, 1960) and leaders (Curtin, 1975; Robinson, 1985), specific time frames (Barry, 1997; Quinn, 1972), isolated episodes or empires (Hanson & Robinson, 1991; Oloruntimehin, 1972), or particular ethnic groups (Hansen, 1996).

Gomez's (2018) *African Dominion* is a seminal work on West African history and the growth of Islam in the region. However, it focuses primarily on the ancient kingdoms of Ghana, Mali, and Songhay, and only briefly addresses leadership in neighboring states, such as the Hausa kingdoms. This study fills a significant gap by examining the rulership of West African Muslim Caliphs across space and time within a single work. Rather than comparing African Islamic leaders to those outside the continent, I compare them to other Muslim leaders within the same region and continent.

Notably, Muslim leaders in West Africa have a long history of engaging in political affairs, not only within their territories and neighboring kingdoms but also with distant peoples and empires. Their interactions were not limited to European powers such as France, England, Portugal, and Spain, but also extended to the Mamluk Empire in Egypt (Gomez, 2018), the Ottoman Empire in Istanbul (Calbreath, 2023), and others. As Muslim leaders, they routinely interacted with peoples and states of different faiths. This raises the question: What

INTRODUCTION

leadership lessons can be drawn from their experiences, and how might we apply their successes to today's pluralistic environment?

African caliphs had to manage both internal and external conflicts, each with the potential to threaten their rule. Domestically, issues such as succession disputes, taxation, and religious administration were common. Even seemingly minor matters could have significant and lasting effects. For example, Mansa Sulayman (d. 1539) of the Malian Empire, in attempting to divorce his wife, Kassi, who was his cousin and had widespread support, triggered a costly civil war (Gomez, 2018). Personal relationships, therefore, were as crucial as maintaining a thriving economy or ensuring food security. As Bueno de Mesquita et al. (2002) note, domestic issues often influence foreign policy decisions. The same was true for African caliphs during West Africa's Classical Islamic period. Many sought expansionist policies, with religion often serving as a rallying cry for an aggressive foreign policy. Islamic scholars and an increasingly Islamized population were key forces pushing caliphs to spread Islam into regions that still adhered to traditional religions. Furthermore, caliphs frequently clashed over several issues, including secession, territorial disputes, and concerns about the piety of fellow rulers.

The question of whether caliphs governed pious nations was of significant concern. For instance, Sheikh Usman dan Fodio's (d. 1817) revolution was partly motivated by his disillusionment with the corrupt and un-Islamic behavior of many Muslim political leaders (Last, 1967). A similar rationale informed Sheikh al-Hajj Umar Tall's (d. 1865) revolt against Muslim communities in Masina and Segu (Willis, 1989). Maba Diakhou (d. 1867), in the present-day Senegambian region, offers another example. After installing Macodou (d. 1863) as the leader of his newly conquered province, Maba Diakhou withdrew his support when Macodou celebrated by engaging in heavy drinking, which is prohibited in Islam. Macodou was subsequently ousted (Quinn, 1972).

In examining the political legacy of Islamic leaders in West Africa, it is essential to consider the influence of Islam's Prophet Muhammad (may Peace Be Upon Him). African caliphs, unfamiliar with the political theories of Machiavelli or Hobbes, were well-versed in the leadership qualities, attributes, and wisdom of Muhammad. As will be explored in subsequent chapters, Muhammad's personalist leadership established a stable model for future rulers. For African caliphs, leadership was rooted in the example set by Muhammad. He not only gathered the first Muslim community but also established the first Islamic state, which grew to encompass much of modern-day Saudi Arabia. Muhammad faced many of the same political challenges that confront leaders today, including issues of taxation, diplomacy, war, and social matters such as divorce, inheritance, and economic development. African caliphs studied Muhammad's biography, Islamic rulings, and hadith literature to guide their decision-making, often equating success with adherence to Islam and failure with deviation from it. While some caliphs sought to emulate Muhammad's political pragmatism, others adhered strictly to his example of Islamic practice, and still others invoked Islam only when politically convenient. The implications of these varied approaches are explored throughout this study.

The following chapters offer a deeper understanding of the political leadership of African caliphs. Chapter 2 introduces the theory of personalist rule as it applies to Muslim leadership in Islamic West Africa. It outlines the context of the current work within the broader literature on political leadership and demonstrates how this study fills gaps in understanding why

INTRODUCTION

African leaders in Islamic West Africa should be considered exemplary sources of leadership in the broader field of political studies, particularly in the context of Black political leadership. Chapter 3 discusses the concept of the caliphate in West Africa, tracing its evolution from the death of Prophet Muhammad in 7th-century Arabia to its distinctive development in West Africa. It focuses on the establishment of caliphates and the adaptation of Islamic practices by local rulers. The chapter highlights key figures such as Sundiatta Keita (d. 1255) and Mansa Musa (d. 1337) to offer deeper insights. Additionally, it examines how African caliphs interacted with indigenous African traditions. Chapter 4 examines the rulership of West African caliphs, focusing on how these leaders were able to acquire political power against significant odds. This chapter examines how spiritual authority influenced political power among African Caliphs, offering historical examples that highlight the intersection of religion and governance. Chapter 5 explores the factors that contributed to the long-term political stability of West African caliphs. In this section, I analyze the political strategies employed by these rulers, emphasizing their use of religion, diplomacy, and strategic thinking to maintain power. Chapter 6 investigates the conditions that led to the decline of Caliphal power and authority. This chapter provides a comprehensive examination of the factors that contributed to the loss of power among African Caliphs during West Africa's Classical Islamic period, focusing on internal political dynamics such as familial disputes, strategic errors, and Islamic reform movements, alongside the external pressures of colonial encroachment. I include case studies of rulers such as Askia Muhammad (d. 1538) and Mai Ahmad (d. 1808) to illustrate how personal ambition, poor judgment, and revolutionary forces often led to the downfall of these leaders. Each chapter concludes with a summary of findings and reflections on how this work can assist contemporary political thinkers and activists.

One central aim of this study is to argue that the leadership scholarship of present-day Black leaders is incomplete without a deeper understanding of how their ancestors governed. Muslim African leaders of the past contended with Arabs, Europeans, other African tribes, various religions, and both domestic and international economic forces, challenges that continue to resonate in the politics of African descendants today. By studying the actions of past African leaders, contemporary leaders can gain insights that may help inform their approaches to the problems of governance today.

REFERENCES

Adeleye, R. A. (1971). *Power and diplomacy in Northern Nigeria, 1804–1906: The Sokoto Caliphate and its enemies.* London.

Alford, T. (2007). *Prince among slaves: The true story of an African prince sold into slavery in the American South* (30th anniversary ed.). Oxford: Oxford University Press.

Association of Black Women Historians, Terborg-Penn, R., Harley, S., & Rushing, A. B. (1989). *Women in Africa and the African diaspora.* Howard University Press.

Austin, A. (2012). *African Muslims in antebellum America: Transatlantic stories and spiritual struggles.* New York, NY: Routledge.

Barry, B. (1997). *Senegambia and the Atlantic slave trade.* Cambridge: Cambridge University Press.

Brenner, L. (1973). *The Shehus of Kukawa: A history of the Al-Kanemi dynasty of Bornu.* Clarendon Press: Oxford.

Calbreath, D. (2023). *The sergeant: The incredible life of Nicholas Said: Son of an African general, slave of the Ottomans, free man under the Tsars, hero of the Union Army.* Pegasus Books.

Charles, E. A. (1977). *Precolonial Senegal: The Jolof Kingdom, 1800–1890* (African Research Studies, no. 12). Boston: African Studies Center, Boston University.

INTRODUCTION

Curtin, P. (1975). Economic change in precolonial Africa: Senegambia in the era of the slave trade. *Journal of the Historical Society of Nigeria, 8*(4), 173–176.

Curtin, P. (1971). Jihad in West Africa: Early phases and inter-relations in Mauritania and Senegal. *The Journal of African History, 12*(1), 11–24.

de Mesquita, B. B., Morrow, J. D., Siverson, R. M., & Smith, A. (2002). Political institutions, policy choice and the survival of leaders. *British Journal of Political Science, 32*(4), 559–590.

De Pizan, C. (1982|1405). *The book of the city of ladies* (J. Richards, Trans.). New York: Persea Books.

Diouf, S. A. (1998). *Servants of Allah: African Muslims enslaved in the Americas*. New York, NY: New York University Press.

Gomez, M. A. (2018). *African dominion: A new history of empire in early and medieval West Africa*. Princeton, NJ: Princeton University Press.

Gomez, M. (1992). *Pragmatism in the age of jihad: The precolonial state of Bundu*. Cambridge: Cambridge University Press.

Gomez, M. (2019). *Reversing sail: A history of the African diaspora*. New York: Cambridge University Press.

Hamilton, A., Madison, J., & Jay, J. (2005). *The Federalist Papers*. New York: Signet Classics.

Hanson, J., & Robinson, D. (Eds. & Trans.). (1991). *After the jihad: The reign of Ahmad al-Kabir in the Western Sudan* (African Historical Sources, no. 2). East Lansing.

Hanson, J. (1996). *Migration, jihad, and Muslim authority in West Africa: The Futanke colonies in Kaarta*. Bloomington and Indianapolis: Indiana University Press.

Herskovits, M. J. (1941). *The myth of the negro past*. Harpers.

Johnston, H. A. S. (1966). *A selection of Hausa stories*. Oxford: Clarendon Press.

Klein, M. (1968). *Islam and imperialism in Senegal: Sine-Saloum, 1847–1914*. Hoover Institution on War, Revolution, and Peace.

Last, M. (1967). *The Sokoto Caliphate*. New York: Humanities Press.

Levtzion, N., & Hopkins, J. F. P. (2011). *Corpus of early Arabic sources for West African history*. Markus Wiener Publishers: Princeton.

Machiavelli, N., & Bull, G. (2003). *The prince*. Penguin Classics.

Oloruntimehin, B. O. (1972). *The Segu Tukulor Empire*. New York: Humanities Press.

Quinn, C. (1972). *Mandingo kingdoms of the Senegambia*. Evanston: Northwestern University Press.

Rodney, W. (1970). *A history of the Upper Guinea Coast: 1545–1800*. New York: Monthly Review Press.

Sudarkasa, N. (1986). The status of women in indigenous African societies. *Feminist Studies, 12*(1), 91–103.

Turner, L. (1949). *Africanisms in the Gullah dialect*. Chicago: University of Chicago Press.

Walters, R., & Smith, R. (1999). *African American leadership*. Albany, NY: State University of New York Press.

Woodson, C. G. (1939|2016). *African heroes and heroines* (Reprint ed., The Woodson Series). Baltimore, MD: Black Classic Press.

Woodson, C. G. (1990). *The mis-education of the Negro*. Trenton, NJ: Africa World Press.

CHAPTER 2

THE CALIPHATE IN ISLAMIC WEST AFRICA

The Almaamy Umar of the Imamate of Futa Jallon in *Voyage de Lambert au Fuuta Jallon in 1860. Tour du Monde*, p.395

CHAPTER 2

THE CALIPHATE IN WEST AFRICA: A PRIMER

West Africa is a vast region located on the world's second-largest and second-most populous continent. To provide some context, the entire continental United States can fit within the boundaries of West Africa. Islam has had a significant presence in Africa since its early days, beginning when members of Prophet Muhammad's community fled to Abyssinia, seeking protection from the Negus (king) against Arab tribes hostile to the new religion (Haykal, 1976). The early Muslim flight to the powerful African kingdom is known as Islam's first *hijira* or emigration (Ali, 1993). Among the Companions of Prophet Muhammad who fled to Abyssinia were Uthman (Islam's third Caliph), Ali (Prophet Muhammad's son-in-law and Islam's fourth Caliph), and Fatima (the Prophet's daughter). King Najashi (also known as Ashama) of Abyssinia not only offered them protection but also became the first monarch in the world to accept Islam. Although his conversion was personal and did not result in the conversion of his kingdom, he allowed the early Muslim community to grow and thrive in a safe environment. Today, Abyssinia is subsumed within the modern nations of Ethiopia and Eritrea, with Ethiopia having a larger Muslim population than Iraq.

THE AFRICAN CALIPHS

An African woman was also the first person to lay hands on Prophet Muhammad. Umm Baraka, an Abyssinian, served as the midwife and attendant to Prophet Muhammad's mother, Amina. When Amina gave birth to Muhammad, it was Umm Baraka who successfully assisted in delivering him and gave him his first bath.

When discussing the spread of Islam, one often refers to the Arab conquest. However, this term is both inaccurate and misleading. Scholars are now correcting historians by using the term "Muslim conquest" because the Muslim armies included not only Arabs but also Africans, Persians, and other peoples, all united in their zeal for the triumph of Islam. Numerous other examples highlight Africa's role in early Islam, making it clear that the history of Islam is deeply intertwined with Africa. Today, Africa is the only continent with a Muslim majority. According to Ware (2014), Muslims in Africa represent 27% of the global Muslim population, with most of Africa's Muslims residing in Sub-Saharan Africa. While 164 million Muslims live in North Africa, over 273 million Muslims live south of the Sahara, constituting more than one-sixth of the world's Muslim population (Ware, 2014). Thus, Islam not only serves as a religion for the majority in Africa but also as a comprehensive guide for life and leadership.

Given that Prophet Muhammad was an Arab who lived and died in Arabia, one might question whether a caliphate could even exist in West Africa. This section begins with this fundamental inquiry. Muslims regard Prophet Muhammad as the final Prophet and Messenger of Allah (God). This exalted status was unique to Muhammad. After his death, however, instead of passing on the title of the final Prophet, the office of the caliph (or vice-regent) was established. The caliph was designated as Muhammad's deputy on Earth. Following Muhammad's death, his close friend and advisor, Abu Bakr, was chosen as the first caliph. The first four caliphs are collectively known as the Rashidun Caliphate, or the Rightly Guided Caliphs. After this period, the succession became increasingly contested and convoluted, and by the Middle Ages, the caliphate's authority largely dissipated. As Nobili (2020) notes, "the title khalifa became somewhat devalued in the course of the Middle Ages, in that it was used increasingly by local Muslim rulers who had no serious claim to worldwide authority" (p. 7). According to Nobili (2020), the "true and significance of the terms caliph and caliphate lies in the fact that both of them imply absolute rejection of the secular and profane… [kingship and king]" (p. 7).

As Islam spread throughout West Africa, Islamic political leaders began to adopt Islamic titles, gradually replacing traditional ones. In some cases, they used both simultaneously. This shift was a reflection of their growing identification as Muslim leaders of Islamic states rather than as secular or traditional rulers. The titles adopted varied based on region, religious doctrine, ethnicity, and other factors. For example, in the Senegambian region, Fulani political leaders adopted the title *Almaamy*, a local pronunciation of the Arabic term *Al-Imam*. In Borno, political leaders used the title *Shehu*, distinguishing themselves from traditional rulers known as *Mais*. *Shehu* is another way of saying *Sheikh* in Arabic. I thus employ the terms "Caliph" and "Caliphate" for African Muslim rulers and polities due to their rejection of secular identification and embrace of an Islamic identity generally.

Many narratives about the introduction of Islam in West Africa begin with the arrival of Muslim Arab and Berber merchants in the Sahel, who engaged in lucrative trade with the Ghanaian Empire to the south. Some accounts suggest the Moorish Almoravid movement, which allegedly conquered the Ghanaian Empire and imposed Islam by force. In both cases, the Ghanaian Empire is central to these origin stories of Islam in West Africa. However, as I will discuss below, the narrative of the Almoravid conquest of Ghana has been debunked (Sanneh, 2016). The more plausible narrative involves Arab and Berber merchants, though this account remains incomplete. Alongside the merchants, scholars and clerics often traveled in large caravans (Levtzion & Pouwels, 2000). These clerics played a crucial role in making Islam appealing to the people they encountered along their trade routes throughout Western Sudan. Levtzion and Pouwels note, "It was through them that Islam actually left traces along the trade routes… Clerics followed the merchants to the commercial towns, where they served the Muslim community as imams and teachers. The clerics became integrated into African societies by playing religious, social, and political roles" (Levtzion & Pouwels, 2000, p. 38). As Lamin Sanneh and others have documented, Islam's spread in West Africa was a peaceful endeavor (Sanneh, 2016; Sanneh, 1989).

CALIPHS IN WEST AFRICA

The first Muslim Caliph in West Africa was War Dyabe (also known as War-Ndyay), the king of Takrur, who died around 1040/1041 (Levtzion, 1980). According to Levtzion (1980), War Dyabe's conversion to Islam preceded the Islamization of Ghana, which occurred between 1076 and 1102. Once War Dyabe embraced Islam, his subjects followed suit, adopting the faith in large numbers (Levtzion, 1980). Thus, Islam reached the upper echelons of Black West Africa well before the Almoravid revolution in the 1050s (Sanneh, 2016). While the precise beginning of Ghana's Islamization remains uncertain, it is generally accepted that the process unfolded peacefully in the 12th century, further reinforced by the Almoravid movement (Sanneh, 2016). In contrast, modern-day Turkey was not Islamized until the 15th century.

Another early Caliph of West Africa was Sundiatta Keita (d. 1255) of the Malian Empire. Niane's (1965) classic epic of Sundiatta provides a comprehensive retelling of this significant African figure, and I will not repeat the narrative here. However, several key points warrant mention. Sundiatta was not Mali's first Muslim ruler; his father and grandfather were both Muslim chiefs. In tracing Sundiatta's Islamic lineage, Levtzion (1980) refers to an oral tradition recorded by Ibn Khaldun, which identifies Barmandana as the first Muslim king of Mali, approximately 10 generations prior to Sundiatta. This Islamic legacy persisted through the Keita clan, influencing both Sundiatta and his successors. During Sundiatta's reign, Mali was still a relatively small chiefdom within the larger Ghanaian Empire. Although some have suggested that Mali became a Muslim state following the Almoravid invasion, there is insufficient evidence to confirm that Ghana was actually defeated by the Almoravids (Conrad & Fisher, 1982). In their detailed analysis of the principal sources on ancient Ghana's history, Conrad and Fisher (1982) find no evidence of a conquest by the Almoravids. This assertion contrasts with the later scholarly consensus, which mistakenly took the idea of an Almoravid conquest as a given. As Conrad and Fisher (1982) observe, the relationship between the Almoravids and the Muslims of the Sudan appears to have been one of mutual cooperation, not conquest: "The relationship... seems on the whole to reflect a more-or-less equal partnership between the Almoravids and the Muslims of the Sudan" (p. 25). The authors further note that if there was any power imbalance, Ghana was likely the superior entity, with the Almoravids in a subordinate role.

Ghana had become well-Islamized by the time of its eventual downfall, although not all of its people embraced Islam. The decline of Ghana in the 13th century was precipitated by the rise of the Susu, who had traditionally served as slaves to the royal families and prominent figures in Ghana. Many in the Susu community resisted abandoning their traditional beliefs. When Sundiatta ascended to the Malian throne, he defeated the Susu ruler, Sumanguru, who was known for his adherence to traditional religion. Sumanguru's resistance to Islam continued until his death. Following his victory, Sundiatta centered the new kingdom of Mali, which succeeded Ghana as the dominant empire in West Africa, becoming one of the largest empires in the world. The legacy of the Malian Empire is significant both in African and Islamic history. Sundiatta's grandson, Mansa Abu Bakr, embarked on an extraordinary expedition to the Americas (Van Sertima, 1977), while another grandson, Mansa Musa, became globally renowned for his legendary pilgrimage (Hajj) to Mecca. To this day, both Mansa Abu Bakr and Mansa Musa are considered among the wealthiest individuals in history. As we will discuss later, Mansa Musa's reign was pivotal for the caliphate in West Africa because of his refusal to acknowledge the sovereignty or Islamic leadership of any other ruler or state (Gomez, 2018). Under Musa, Mali positioned itself as an independent Islamic kingdom, connected to the Middle East solely through the sacred sites of Mecca and Medina. Each subsequent ruler of Mali was Muslim, and with each new reign, the empire became increasingly devoted to Islam.

However, after a period of internal decay, fratricide, and political instability, the Malian Empire eventually lost its dominance in West Africa. The Songhay Empire emerged as the new hegemon, with its capital in Gao. The Songhay Empire, too, was a Muslim state. Za-Kassi, the fifteenth king of Songhay, converted to Islam around 1009–1010 of his own volition, without external compulsion (Arnold, 1912). Later, the legendary Sonni Ali (d. 1492) ascended the Songhay throne, and under his rule, the empire expanded significantly, though Sonni Ali was not particularly devoted to Islam. Despite his personal ambivalence, his conquests spread Islam throughout the empire. Following Sonni Ali's death, Askia Muhammad (d. 1538) ascended to power after overthrowing the former's son. A devout Muslim, Askia Muhammad further expanded both Islam and the Songhay Empire. His military campaigns extended the empire's reach as far as Hausaland, and by this time, the Songhay Empire was one of the largest and wealthiest in the world.

After the decline of the northern half of the Songhay Empire in the 16th century, smaller Muslim kingdoms began to form. In the 17th century, Fulani Muslims and revolutionaries established Imamates in regions such as Bundu, Futa Toro, and Futa Jallon. These areas were among the first to adopt state structures governed by Sharia (Islamic law). By the time the northern half of the Songhay Empire had fallen, Islam had become the dominant religion throughout much of West Africa, from the Upper Senegal River Valley to nearly all of the Niger River basin. European explorers' travel accounts, including those of Molien (1820), Barth (1860), and Denham and Clapperton (1826), attest to this widespread Islamization. By this time, Islam had become so deeply integrated into the social fabric of West African life that many of the Islamic revolutions of the late 18th and early 19th centuries were waged against rulers who were themselves Muslim (Lovejoy, 2016).

FALL OF THE NORTHERN HALF OF THE SONGHAY EMPIRE

To provide context for the aftermath of the Moroccan invasion of the Songhay Empire, it is important to examine key events following the attack. In 1594, Pasha Mahmud, the Moroccan military governor, was beheaded by troops loyal to Askia Nuh of the Songhay Empire. Askia Nuh (r. 1592–1599) sent Pasha Mahmud's head to the King of Kebbi, who displayed it in the marketplace for all to see. Soon after, the Moroccan army, having suffered heavy losses, abandoned their efforts in the southern region of the Songhay Empire. This episode helps correct a commonly told narrative of African history. The usual account asserts that the Songhay Empire collapsed entirely following the Moroccan invasion of 1591 and that this marked the end of Songhay's prominence. As a result, discussions on West African history often shift immediately to the Transatlantic Slave Trade. However, the story of Songhay did not end there.

The Songhay Empire, like Rome, was vast and had multiple centers of power. When the eastern half of the Roman Empire fell at Constantinople, the western half continued to exist. Similarly, although the northern half of Songhay fell, Askia Ishaq Dawud (d. 1592) ordered the evacuation of Gao, relocating the empire's capital to the southern regions, including areas such as Dendi and Kano. The Moroccan forces launched several expeditions to force these regions to submit to the Sultan. However, as with the execution of Pasha Mahmud, Moroccan soldiers frequently met their demise. One chronicler notes, "In the 30 years after their victory in 1591, the al-Mansur continued to send arquebusiers to fight the Askiyas, totaling up to 23,000 men by 1604, of whom only 500 returned to Marrakesh. The rest died in battle, succumbed to disease, or were among the few hundred survivors garrisoned in the cities of Djenné, Timbuktu, and Gao" (Samuel, 2022). Thus, neither the Askiyas of Songhay, the Kantas of Kebbi, nor any other major Islamic states south of Songhay-north (except for Bornu) recognized Morocco as their sovereign. Instead, they consistently resisted Moroccan attempts at conquest. The rulers of the southern regions of the Songhay Empire remained independent until the arrival of the French. In fact, Songhay persisted for another 100 years after the Moroccan invasion. During this period, numerous developments occurred: guerrilla campaigns were waged against Moroccan forces and their mercenaries, neighboring communities were incorporated and converted to Islam, and political dynamics shifted. The politics of one of the world's wealthiest and most powerful Islamic empires continued, albeit within a new political framework. The Caliphs of West Africa maintained their sovereignty and authority, often creating new Islamic states in the process.

As mentioned earlier, Fulani rulers and Muslim revolutionaries were among the first in West Africa to establish true Imamates or caliphates, where Islamic rule largely replaced traditional governance (Gomez, 1992; Lovejoy, 2016). The Fulanis were also instrumental in translating the Qur'an into their native language (Sanneh, 1989), which allowed Fulani clerics to study the Qur'an more effectively and strengthened their engagement with Islamic scholarship. The southern half of the Songhay Empire coincided with the spread and entrenchment of Islam in regions like modern-day northern Nigeria, northern Ghana, and other areas. After the Moroccan invasion, Islamic teachers and leaders found refuge in places such as Hausaland (modern-day northern Nigeria), where they established new schools, mosques, and centers of learning. In this way, the southern portion of the Songhay Empire likely served as a critical hub for the dissemination of Islam. Rather than hindering the spread of Islam, the Moroccan invasion of Songhay may have, in many ways, accelerated its expansion in West Africa.

It is also important to recognize that the form of Islam practiced in West Africa often differed from its practice in Arabia. Since the time of Sundiata and even earlier, Islam in West Africa had to adapt to and coexist with local social and religious structures that had been the foundation of African societies for centuries (Sanneh, 2016). Many Islamic scholars fail to distinguish between Arab culture and Islamic culture, tending to dichotomize Muslim rulers as either secular or religious based on how close their praxis and scholarship resemble Arab Muslims. This approach overlooks the diversity of Muslims around the world and the example set by Prophet Muhammad (PBUH), who, after the Treaty of Hudaybiyyah (al Faruqi & al Faruqi, 2014), made peace with his enemies and recognized other religious traditions, such as Judaism and Christianity. This distinction is crucial for understanding the complexity of Islamic rule in West Africa, where tolerance and cohabitation with other religious practices were often central. Some scholars have even questioned the Islamic legitimacy of figures such as Sundiata and Mansa Musa due to their tolerance of other faiths within their domains. However, the broader legacy of Islam in West Africa underscores the fact that Islam has been a significant part of the region for over a millennium, with African rulers embracing the faith from its early days. Contrary to the myth that Islam is foreign to Africa, this analysis challenges such claims, highlighting the African contributions to the faith from its very foundation.

REFERENCES

al Fārūqī, I. R., & al Fārūqī, L. L. (2014). *The Qur'an and the Sunnah*. International Institute of Islamic Thought.

Ali, M. M. (1993). *Muhammad the prophet*. Ahmadiyya Anjuman Ishaat Islam.

Arnold, T. W. (1913). *The preaching of Islam: A history of the propagation of the Muslim faith*. C. Scribner's Sons.

Barth, H. (1860). *Travels and discoveries in North and Central Africa*. J.W. Bradley.

Conrad, D., & Fisher, H. (1982). The conquest that never was: Ghana and the Almoravids, 1076. I. The external Arabic sources. *History in Africa, 9*, 21–59.

Denham, D. (1826). *Narrative of travels and discoveries in Northern and Central Africa, in the years 1822, 1823, and 1824, by Major Denham, Captain Clapperton, and the late Doctor Oudney*. John Murray.

Gomez, M. A. (2018). *African dominion: A new history of empire in early and medieval West Africa*. Princeton University Press.

Gomez, M. (1992). Pragmatism in the age of jihad: The precolonial state of Bundu. *Cambridge University Press*.

Haykal, M. (1976). *The life of Muhammad*. Islamic Book Trust.

Levtzion, N. (1980). *Ancient Ghana and Mali*. Africana Publishing Company.

Levtzion, N., & Pouwels, R. (2000). *The history of Islam in Africa*. Ohio University Press.

Lovejoy, P. E. (2016). *Jihād in West Africa during the age of revolutions* (1st ed.). Ohio University Press.

Mollien, G. T., Berthier, P., Eyriès, J. B. B., Shackell, W., & Colburn, H. (1820). *Travels in the interior of Africa, to the sources of the Senegal and Gambia: Performed by command of the French Government, in the year 1818* (T. E. Bowdich, Ed.). Henry Colburn & Co.

Niane, D. T. (1965). *Sundiata: An epic of old Mali*. Longmans.

Samuels, I. (2022). Morocco, Songhai, Bornu and the quest to create an African empire to rival the Ottomans: An ambitious sultan's dream of a Trans-Atlantic, Trans-Saharan empire. *African History Extra*. https://www.africanhistoryextra.com/p/morocco-songhai-bornu-and-the-quest

Sanneh, L. (2016). *Beyond jihad: The pacifist tradition in West African Islam*. Oxford University Press.

Sanneh, L. (1989). *The Jakhanke Muslim clerics: A religious and historical study of Islam in Senegambia*. University Press of America.

Ware, R. (2014). *The walking Qur'an: Islamic education, embodied knowledge, and history in West Africa*. University of North Carolina Press.

Van Sertima, I. (1977). *They came before Columbus: The African presence in ancient America*. Random House.

CHAPTER 3

THEORY OF PERSONALIST RULE IN ISLAMIC WEST AFRICA

Almaamy Samori Toure of the Wassallou Empire

CHAPTER 3

THEORY OF PERSONALIST RULE IN ISLAMIC WEST AFRICA

This chapter offers a compelling approach to understanding the political dynamics of West African Caliphs through the concept of personalist rule. Drawing on historical examples, I illustrate the complexities of governance in a religious and politically charged context. By examining the interaction between individual rulers and their strategic use of Islam in their pursuit of political power, I show how the concept of personalist rule can deepen our understanding of Islamic rulership in West Africa.

I classify West African Caliphs within the framework of personalist rule, a political system in which "rivalries and struggles of powerful and willful men, rather than impersonal institutions, ideologies, public policies, or class interests, are fundamental in shaping political life" (Jackson & Rosberg, 1984, p. 421). Personalist rule primarily centers on individual rulers and their exercise of power. The main independent variable in this study is rulership: the practice of power among individual leaders. Jackson and Rosberg (1984) further describe personal rule as "an elitist political system composed of the privileged and powerful few in which the many are usually unmobilized, unorganized, and therefore relatively powerless to command the attention and action of government. The system favors the ruler and his allies and clients: its essential activity involves gaining access to a personal regime's patronage or displacing the ruler and perhaps his regime and installing another" (p. 424). While each ruler in this study identifies as Muslim, the extent to which they adhere to Islamic principles of rulership and governance, or incorporate Islamic practices into their personal lives, varies. West African Caliphs frequently employed Islam to advance their personal and strategic interests, though their success depended on their political acumen.

Although the rulers in this study identify with Islam (or at least nominally), I refrain from categorizing the political systems they governed as theocracies. A theocracy is defined as "government by a clergy, or a self-appointed group who claim to speak and act on God's behalf" (Ferrero, 2013, p. 723). While some of the Caliphs in this study emerged from clerical backgrounds, few claimed to speak or act as divine representatives. Exceptions exist, such as Shaykh al-Hajj Umar Tall (d. 1864), but, by and large, these Caliphs should be viewed as political contestants rather than as divinely authorized rulers.

A key assumption in this study is that all the Caliphs under examination were, in fact, personalist rulers. I draw on Machiavelli's (2003) approach, which focuses on whether rulers are effective or ineffective, rather than Jackson and Rosberg's (1984) categorization of personalist rulers into four distinct types: prince, autocrat, prophet, and tyrant. My analysis does not seek to determine the effectiveness of these rulers, but rather to identify practices that likely influenced outcomes. Specifically, I examine factors that contributed to the acquisition, maintenance, and loss of Caliphal power.

The Caliphal system represents a form of personalist rule, but this does not imply that the Caliph rules arbitrarily.

THEORY OF PERSONALIST RULE IN ISLAMIC WEST AFRICA

Generally, a Caliph must balance the implementation of Islam with the political power necessary to maintain his authority. During the Classical Islamic Period of West Africa, Islam served as a constraining force on the ruler's power. As with most religions, Islam imposes binding obligations on its followers, and for political leaders, the religion confers significant duties and responsibilities (Fudi, 1983). The principles of good governance and rule are outlined in the Qur'an and the Sunnah of Prophet Muhammad (PBUH), which serve as the primary sources of Islamic jurisprudence. The oppressive rule of certain Caliphs in West Africa prompted political reform efforts by devout Muslims, who often replaced their former rulers. Notable reformers such as Karamokho Alfa (d. 1751), Ibrahima Sori (d. 1784), and Sheikh Usman dan Fodio (d. 1817) were among those who sought to challenge these regimes. Other reformers chose to secede from these tyrannical rulers, establishing independent kingdoms of their own.

A ruler's level of faith determines the degree to which he feels constrained by these religious duties. Non-observant rulers, however, make themselves vulnerable to reform-minded forces both within and outside their realms. Even non-pious Caliphs, therefore, publicly embraced Islam and extolled its virtues. Sunni Ali of the Songhay Empire, for example, was known for tolerating traditional religious practices, despite the Empire officially being a Muslim state. He was also criticized for his lax approach to Islamic observance, often performing his five obligatory prayers all at once at the end of the day, even when no obstacles prevented him from praying on time. Nevertheless, he performed the prayers daily. After his death, his son assumed the throne but mistakenly continued his father's accommodation of traditional religions. This decision ultimately led to a confrontation with one of the Empire's most pious military commanders. Conversely, strict adherence to

Islamic practices, while potentially aiding in the acquisition of power, could also provoke internal unrest and external intervention. A ruler's rigid application of Islamic law might incite revolts or prompt foreign powers to view the regime as a threat to their survival (Gomez, 1992).

A Caliph's foreign and domestic policies, along with their public adherence to Islam, thus become central to their leadership survival. This dynamic mirrors the political theories described by Bueno de Mesquita and Alistair Smith (2010), who argue that political leaders must control and satisfy key coalitions for effective governance. African Caliphs, however, also often engaged in the removal or replacement of important coalitions to secure their power. Sunni Ali, for example, recognized the critical role of the *ulama* (the learned community) in shaping public opinion. Due to their dissatisfaction with his half-hearted commitment to Islam, segments of the *ulama* allied with the Empire's enemies, openly condemning Sunni Ali and seeking assistance from external forces to overthrow him. Rather than attempting to appease or control these important groups in regions such as Jenne and Timbuktu, Sunni Ali executed many *ulama* and replaced them with scholars more aligned with his views (Gomez, 2018).

In contrast, other African Caliphs sought to influence the *ulama* through intellectual campaigns. Shaykh al-Hajj Umar Tall, for instance, engaged in a public intellectual debate with Ahmad al-Bakkai al-Kunti of the Qadari Sufi order (Robinson, 1985; Willis, 1989). Al-Hajj Umar Tall accused Ahmad al-Bakkai al-Kunti of losing his credibility as a true believer due to his support for non-Muslim violence against Tall's military expeditions (Willis, 1989). Al-Kunti, on the other hand, critiqued Tall's jihad as a pursuit of personal ambition and wealth, alleging that Tall sought excuses to justify the killing and enslaving of Muslims for material gain. This intellectual exchange was crucial for both figures, as they were influential in shaping West African Islamic politics. For al-Hajj Umar Tall, discrediting al-Kunti was vital to gaining the support of Muslims seeking Islamic reform. For al-Kunti, exposing Tall as a fraudulent leader helped prevent his followers from joining Tall's jihad.

Another example of a Caliph strategically managing public perception is the case of Sheikhu Ahmadu Lobbo (d. 1845) of the Caliphate of Massina (Hamdullahi). As noted by Nobili (2020), Lobbo inserted himself into the *Tarikh al-Fattash* and portrayed himself as the long-awaited Renewer of the Faith. By altering every available copy of the *Tarikh al-Fattash* to include this claim, Lobbo sought to strengthen the legitimacy of his revolution and cement his place in Islamic history as an important figure. In a similar vein, the leaders of the Sokoto Caliphate engaged in an intellectual debate with Sheikh Muhammad al-Amin al-Kanemi (d. 1837), who represented the Mai/ruler of Borno over the legitimacy of the Sokoto jihad against Muslim states, with both sides aiming to influence the *ulama* in the region.

Though leaders within the personalist regimes examined in this study often assume various titles (e.g., Almaamy, Brak, Kanta, Amir), they are generally classified as authoritarian. Jackson and Rosberg (1982) define authoritarianism as "an arbitrary and usually personal government that uses law and the coercive instruments of the state to expedite its own purposes of monopolizing power, while denying the political rights and opportunities of other groups to compete for that power" (p. 23). They further note that personal rule is characterized by the "removal of constitutional rights and protections from political opponents, the elimination of institutional checks and balances, and the centralization and concentration of state power" (Jackson & Rosberg, 1982, pp. 23–24). Geddes, Wright, and Frantz (2014) identify several types of authoritarian regimes, including "dominant-party, military, personalist, monarchic, oligarchic, indirect military, or hybrids of the first three" (p. 317). These systems differ in terms of whether central state control rests in the hands of a ruling party (dominant-party dictatorships), a royal family (monarchies), the military (military rule), or a narrower group centered around an individual dictator (personalist dictatorships) (Geddes, Wright, & Frantz, 2014, p. 317).

It is important to note that personalist regimes and their rulers vary. Cheibub, Gandhi, and Vreeland (2010) outline three basic types: monarchic dictatorships, military dictatorships, and civilian dictatorships. Military dictatorships depend on military force to assume and retain power, while monarchic dictatorships are based on family and kin networks. Civilian dictatorships are neither military nor monarchic. The personalist rulers discussed in this study govern regimes that span these categories. For example, the Islamic empires of Mali and Songhay were monarchic dictatorships, while many regimes in the Senegambian region, such as those in Futa Toro and Futa Jallon, were primarily civilian, though occasionally transitioning to monarchic. The Sokoto Caliphate and the Toucouleur Empire were also monarchical, whereas the Wassoulou Empire of Samori Ture (d. 1900) was a military dictatorship.

Another key aspect of Africa's Classical Islamic period is its interaction with non-Black groups. Prior to major encounters with Europe, Arab travelers were often regarded as White in much of West Africa. Historically, both Arabs and Europeans were significant sources of ideas, commerce, and conflict for African Caliphs. A careful examination of Islamic West Africa's relationship with external powers highlights the necessity of cultivating strategic alliances with such entities. However, overreliance on a single foreign power can threaten independence. It is important to understand the alliances of one's allies and to develop independent relationships with them. For instance, although Morocco was a key ally of the Songhay Empire, it did not disclose to Songhay that it had been amassing a stockpile of guns and other advanced technologies from European sources. This proved costly when Morocco, confident in its new military capabilities, crossed the Sahara to wage war against the Black kingdoms of West Africa (Diop, 1987). Though Morocco initially succeeded in its campaign against the Songhay Empire, this success was short-lived. Morocco eventually withdrew, but the conflict sparked the creation of additional Islamic states south of the Sahara.

METHODOLOGY AND DATA

This study creates an original dataset based on information from published articles, books, monographs, dissertations, official archives, websites, and other research on Islam and Muslim leaders in West Africa. Using this data, I compile general information about each African Caliph, including their reign years, whether they were killed in office, their location, and other characteristics associated with their leadership. By employing a variety of research tools and relying on a mixture of different sources, I aim to gather the most accurate data possible. Additionally, I conduct a comparative analysis of different African Caliphs from the 11th to the 19th century. The unit of analysis is not the political system or kingdom but the individual ruler. Each step of the analysis is supported by historical cases, which serve to illustrate key points of interest. These illustrations are not intended to evaluate the leaders' actions as entirely right or wrong, but to highlight particular principles of significance. While unconventional, the objective of my methodology is to understand the nature of political power among African Caliphs.

This chapter examines the concept of personalist rule among West African Caliphs, focusing on how individual rulers used Islam to exercise political power. In this context, West

African Caliphs are categorized under personalist rule, where influential individuals, rather than institutions or ideologies, shape political life. These Caliphs employed Islam to further their personal and strategic interests, with varying degrees of adherence to Islamic principles.

REFERENCES

Cheibub, J. A., Gandhi, J., & Vreeland, J. R. (2010). Democracy and dictatorship revisited. *Public Choice*, *143*(1–2), 67–101.

de Mesquita, B. B., & Smith, A. (2010). Leader survival, revolutions, and the nature of government finance. *American Journal of Political Science*, *54*(4), 936–950.

Diop, C. A. (1987). *Precolonial Black Africa: A comparative study of the political and social systems of Europe and Black Africa, from antiquity to the formation of modern states*. L. Hill.

Ferrero, M. (2013). The rise and demise of theocracy: Theory and some evidence. *Public Choice*, *156*(3–4), 723–750.

Fudi, Abdullâhi b. (1983). *Tazyln al-waraqdl* (M. Hiskett, Ed. & Trans.). Ibadan University Press.

Geddes, B., Wright, J., & Frantz, E. (2014). Autocratic breakdown and regime transitions: A new data set. *Perspective on Politics*, *12*(2), 313–331.

Gomez, M. (1992). *Pragmatism in the age of jihad: The precolonial state of Bundu*. Cambridge University Press.

Jackson, R. H., & Rosberg, C. G. (1982). *Personal rule in Black Africa: Prince, autocrat, prophet, tyrant*. University of California Press.

Jackson, R. H., & Rosberg, C. G. (1984). Personal rule: Theory and practice in Africa. *Comparative Politics*, *16*(4), 421–442.

Robinson, D. (1985). *The holy war of Umar Tal: The Western Sudan in the mid-nineteenth century*. Clarendon Press.

Machiavelli, N., & Bull, G. (2003). *The Prince*. Penguin Classics.

Nobili, M. (2020). *Sultan, caliph, and the renewer of the faith: Aḥmad Lobbo, the Tārīkh al-Fattāsh and the making of an Islamic state in West Africa*. Cambridge University Press.

Willis, J. (1989). *In the path of Allah: The passion of Al-Hajj Umar: An essay into the nature of charisma in Islam*. Frank Cass & Co. Ltd.

CHAPTER 4

ACQUIRING CALIPHAL POWER

Sheikh Ahmadou Kabir
Caliph of the Tukulor Empire and son of Sheikh al-Hajj Umar Tall

Voyage dans le Soudan occidental (Senegambie-Niger) by M.E. Mage;
Librarie de L. Hachette, Paris, 1868

CHAPTER 4

PERSONALIST RULE: ACQUIRING CALIPHAL POWER

This chapter examines the factors that led to the acquisition of Caliphal power during the Classical Islamic period in West Africa. It offers a nuanced study of the rise of African Caliphs and the intersection of spiritual and political authority. Examining a diverse group of leaders and their varied methods of acquiring power highlights the dynamic and often turbulent political landscapes in which precolonial West African Islamic leaders navigated.

My analysis reveals several key factors that facilitated the acquisition of Caliphal authority, including military prowess, inheritance, education, piety, and political acumen. High birth and lineage were also important factors in assuming Caliphal power. For instance, each subsequent ruler after the Askia's dynastic founder, Askia al-hajj Muhammad, traces their descent to him. In the Malian Empire, the ruling Caliphs were almost exclusively members of the Keita family, descendants of the empire's founder, Sundjata Keita (Levtzion, 1980). Similarly, in the Sokoto Empire, each ruler was a direct descendant of the Caliphate's founder, Sheikh Usman dan Fodio (Last, 1967).

Rulers from dynastic families also governed in Borno, Bundu, and various other regions of West Africa.

Among the Caliphs discussed, 47% had fathers who were also Caliphs, while 40% had fathers who never ruled, as shown in Table 2. In some regions, the tradition of inherited leadership was particularly strong, though exceptions existed where family members not directly in line for succession managed to acquire the throne. This was especially evident in Hausaland, where 60% of those who attained Caliphal authority through their own efforts had fathers who were also rulers.

Nevertheless, this chapter focuses on Caliphs who ascended to power not through inheritance but through their personal abilities. The factors influencing power acquisition are crucial for understanding the dynamics of leadership in African Islamic societies, especially in regions where traditional religions remain influential. The Caliphs in this chapter (as in other chapters of this study) will not be examined chronologically. Rather, their acquisition of power will be considered in relation to the factors that contributed to their rise. I categorize the modes of power acquisition as follows: a) revolution, b) coup, c) secession, d) election, and d) conversion.

Revolutions are typically defined as organized efforts to overthrow an existing political system. Coups, which can take various forms (e.g., civilian or military), refer to sudden and unlawful seizures of power. In this chapter, I use the term "coup" generically to encompass all such instances. Secession,

PERSONALIST RULE: ACQUIRING CALIPHAL POWER

though increasingly complex in contemporary contexts, generally refers to the withdrawal of political allegiance from a larger political entity to form a new one. The term "election" in this chapter is used in the classical Islamic sense, referring to an organized vote for political authority.

According to Table 1, among the Caliphs who founded Islamic states in West Africa, 48% acquired power through revolutions, while coups were the most common method, accounting for 76%. Approximately 33% became Caliphs through conversion, 19% gained authority through secession, and 15% were elected by prominent groups of electors.

Table 1 Political Events in Which Political Authority Was Acquired Among African Caliphs

How Political Authority Was Acquired?	Percentage
Revolution	48
Coup	76
Secession	19
Conversion	33
Elections	15

Table 2 presents African Caliphs who rose to power through their own means. Several recurring factors are identified in their acquisition of political authority, including a) religious education, b) spiritual authority, and c) courage and means. These factors are briefly discussed below.

Table 2 Caliphs Who Acquired Political Authority by Their Own Means

Caliph	Place	Means of Acquisition	Spiritual Auth.	Islamic Education	Cour. & Means	Father was a Caliph
Abdur-Rahman al-Amin al-Kanemi	Kanem-Bornu Empire	Coup	Low	High	Yes	Yes
Usman dan Fodio	Sokoto Caliphate	Revolution	High	High	Yes	No
Askia al-Hajj Muhammad	Songhay Empire	Coup	High	Middle	Yes	Yes
Sundiatta Keita	Mali Empire	Revolution	Low	Low	Yes	No
Al-Hajj Umar Tall	Tukulor Empire	Revolution	High	High	Yes	No
Sheikhu Ahmadu Lobbo	Caliphate of Hamdullahi	Secession	High	High	Yes	No
Muhammad Bello	Sokoto Caliphate	Election	High	High	Yes	Yes
Askia Muhammad Bonkana Kiyra	Songhay Empire	Election	High	High	Yes	Yes
Suleyman Bal	Imamate of Futo Toro	Revolution	High	High	Yes	No
Abdul Kader Khan	Imamate of Futo Toro	Election	High	High	Yes	No
Karamoka Alfa	Imamate of Futo Djallon	Revolution	High	High	Yes	No
Malik Sy	Imamate of Bundu	Revolution	High	High	Yes	No
Bubu Malik Sy	Imamate of Bundu	Coup	High	High	Yes	Yes
Maka Jiba	Imamate of Bundu	Coup	High	High	Yes	Yes

PERSONALIST RULE: ACQUIRING CALIPHAL POWER

Ruler	Polity	Method				
Amadi Gai	Imamate of Bundu	Coup	High	High	Yes	Yes
Ma Ba Diakha	Kingdom of Rip & Jolof	Revolution	High	High	Yes	No
Muhammad Kanta of Kebbi	Kebbi Empire	Secession	Low	Middle	Yes	No
Askia Ismail	Songhay Empire	Coup	Low	Middle	Yes	Yes
Askia Musa	Songhay Empire	Coup	Low	Middle	Yes	Yes
Sheikh al-Amin al-Kanemi	Kanem-Bornu Empire	Coup	High	High	Yes	No
Samori Toure	Wassalou Empire	Revolution	Low	Low	Yes	No
Mori Ule Sise	Madina	Revolution	High	High	Yes	No
Umme	Kanem-Bornu Empire	Conversion	High	Low		No
Hajj I	Kano Kingdom	Conversion	High	Low	Yes	No
Mamadu Juhe	Hubbu	Secession	High	High	Yes	No
Dan Ayi	Yauri Kingdom	Conversion				
Lawan Babuje	Beddi (or Bade) Kingdom	Inherited	High	High	Yes	Yes
Tenguella	Empire of Great Fula	Secession				
Za Khassi	Songhay Kingdom	Conversion	High	Low	Yes	Yes
Kunburu	Kingdom of Jenne	Conversion	High	Low	Yes	Yes
Mansa Sakura	Empire of Mali	Coup				

43

THE AFRICAN CALIPHS

Caliph	Place	Means of Acquisition	Spiritual Auth.	Islamic Education	Cour. & Means	Father was a Caliph
Mansa Maghan II	Empire of Mali	Coup	High	High	Yes	No
Bokar Biro	Futa Jallon	Coup	High	High	Yes	Yes
Askia Ishaq II	Songhay Empire	Coup	High	High	Yes	Yes
Jal Joop	Cape Verde	Revolution				
Sheikh Amadu Ba	Jollof	Coup	High	High	Yes	No
Albuuri N'jay	Jollof		High	Low	Yes	No
Muhammadu Korau	Katsina Kingdom	Coup	High	High	Yes	Yes
Yaji I	Kano Kingdom	Conversion	High	Low	Yes	Yes
Yauri Jerabana II	Yauri Kingdom	Conversion				
Muhammad Shashere	Kano Kingdom	Election				
Guli	Kano Kingdom	Coup	Low	High	Yes	Yes
Dauda Abasama	Kano Kingdom	Election				Yes
Abubakar Kado	Kano Kingdom	Election				Yes
Muhammadu Zaki	Kano Kingdom	Election				Yes
Bawa	Kano Kingdom	Election				Yes
Kukuna	Kano Kingdom	Coup				Yes

PERSONALIST RULE: ACQUIRING CALIPHAL POWER

Religious Education: Religious education is a dynamic aspect of West African Islam. Muslims pursue education throughout their lives, and thus, I categorize religious training into three levels: high, medium, and low. High-level training refers to clerical education, which was widespread in many parts of West Africa during the Classical Islamic period. Medium-level training indicates strong religious education outside the clerical sphere, often obtained at home or through kinship networks. Low-level training encompasses those who converted to Islam as adults or who, while born Muslim, continued to adhere to traditional religions. This category also includes Muslims with minimal Islamic knowledge or practice.

Most Caliphs in this study (48%) received high-level religious education, making it one of the most consistent factors contributing to the acquisition of Caliphal power. Two percent received medium-level training, and 16% received low-level training. This dynamic is intriguing because it suggests that one need not be a highly learned Islamic scholar to possess spiritual zeal. Religious fervor can significantly impact individuals with minimal religious training. Regardless of their educational background, all Caliphs displayed courage and the means necessary to acquire authority. Even those who seized power through subterfuge or disloyalty exhibited a degree of courage and resourcefulness.

Spiritual Authority: In Islam, spiritual authority is linked to one's proximity to Allah through piety. It encompasses the personal power gained through knowledge, behavior, and respect for the religion. Those with spiritual authority often include religious figures such as clerics, conquerors acting in the name of Islam, or those holding titles like mallam (religious teacher) or qadi (Islamic judge). However, spiritual authority is not limited to individuals with formal religious roles. A person may gain spiritual authority simply by professing devotion to

Islam and governing in accordance with Islamic principles, even without a clerical background. Conversion to Islam and a commitment to spreading the faith can also contribute to spiritual authority.

Courage and Means: Machiavelli once expressed a preference for armed prophets over unarmed ones. Armed prophets, such as Moses, created their own kingdoms and altered the course of history. This distinction is crucial, as seeking political change or the establishment of a new polity is only feasible with both the will and the means to implement it. The challenge of overcoming the classic collective-action problem is often overlooked in discussions of African leadership. In many cases, establishing an Islamic political system in West Africa required the destruction of existing polities and the creation of entirely new ones in their place. Thus, "courage and means" also refers to the resources and organization necessary to achieve such a formidable task.

Table 3 presents African Caliphs who not only gained political authority but also introduced Islam as the state religion. Among the leaders observed, 43% initiated Islam in their respective realms, often through the success of an Islamic revolution or by converting themselves. This does not imply that Islam was entirely absent in these regions before, as in Hausaland, where many deposed leaders were at least nominal Muslims. However, Shehu Usman dan Fodio revitalized the region with a fervent commitment to Islam, requiring all appointed Emirs (governors) to be devout followers. Of the Islamic state initiators, 38% were kings who converted to the faith, and in many cases, their subjects followed suit. This was exemplified by Kunburu, the king of Jenne, who converted to Islam in the late 12th century (Arnold, 1913). Ethnicity also influenced the acquisition of political authority among the Fulanis and Hausas.

PERSONALIST RULE: ACQUIRING CALIPHAL POWER

As shown in Table 3, 38% of the Islam initiators were Fulani, and 23% were Hausa. High Islamic education was also a key characteristic among the initiators of Islam. In fact, more than 52% of these individuals received advanced Islamic education during their youth, as shown in Tables 2 and 3.

Table 3 Caliphs Who Initiated Islamic States

Islamic Initiators	Location
Shehu Usaman dan Fodio	Sokoto Caliphate
Sheikh al-Hajj Umar Tall	Tukulor Empire
Sheikhu Ahmadu Lobo	Massina Caliphate
Suleyman Bal	Imamate of Futa Toro
Karamoka Alfa	Imamate of Futa Jallon
Malik Sy	Imamate of Bundu
Maba Diakhou	Imamate of Rip and Jolof
Muhammad Kanta	Kebbi Kingdom
Samori Ture	Wassoulou Empire
Mori Ule Sise	Madina Kingdom
Umme	Kanem-Borno Empire
Haji I	Kano Kingdom
Mamadu Juhe	Hubbu Kingdom
Dan Ayi	Yauri Kingdom
Lawan Babuje	Beddi Kingdom
Tenguella	Empire of Great Fula
Za Khassi	Songhay Kingdom
Kunburu	Jenne Kingdom
Sultan Abd' Allah	Baghirmi Kingdom
Muhammadu Karau	Katsina Kingdom
Jal Joop	Cape Verde

EDUCATION AND PREPARATION IN YOUTH

Several Caliphs during West Africa's Classical Islamic period ascended to the throne through their own efforts. According to Machiavelli (2003), these individuals could be described as self-made princes. Understanding the exploits of this group is crucial, as they demonstrate the processes by which both religious authority and political power are attained. These Caliphs are significant because, in many cases, they represent the founding generation of their respective empires. Their actions transformed Islam from a marginalized religion practiced by a few into the official state religion, widely embraced by the masses. Some leaders established Islamic polities to provide a safe haven for Muslims to practice their faith without fear of persecution (Ware, 2013). At least one leader sought to create an Islamic state as a strategic base to spread Islam throughout West Africa (Robinson, 1985). In other instances, Islamic rulers engaged in corrupt governance, prompting the formation of new Islamic kingdoms to end oppression (Sulaiman, 2009).

One of the most reform-minded Caliphs of West Africa was Sheikh al-Hajj Umar Tall, the founder of the Tukulor Empire (Oloruntimehin, 1972). At its peak, the Tukulor Empire was among the largest Islamic Caliphates in the world. Tall's preparation for leadership exemplifies the importance of education and discipline in an Islamic polity. He performed Hajj three times (Robinson, 1985; Willis, 1989), a testament to his devotion. Tall's scholarly upbringing also showcased the vast intellectual engagement of Black Africans with Islam. During his journey to perform Hajj, Tall visited Cairo, where he engaged with scholars at the renowned Al-Azhar University (Robinson, 1985). The head scholar at Al-Azhar challenged Tall's knowledge of the Qur'an, but Tall proved superior, reciting the Qur'an flawlessly. He also demonstrated his mastery of the sacred texts of the Tijaniya Order (Robinson, 1985). His intellectual prowess became legendary across the Muslim world. Additionally, Tall trained under his father-in-law, Sultan Muhammad Bello (d. 1837), the Caliph of the Sokoto Caliphate (Adeleye, 1971). Under Sultan Bello, Tall participated in military campaigns to quell rebellions threatening the empire, gaining both administrative and military education from some of the century's most formidable minds.

Tall's extensive travels further enriched his education. He spent considerable time in prominent Islamic centers across Africa and the Middle East. Notably, he visited Sheikhu Ahmadu of the Caliphate of Massina, staying for nine months, and the Borno Empire, where Sheikh Muhammad al-Amin al-Kanemi ruled (Robinson, 1985). Al-Kanemi, a scholarly warrior and statesman, would later prove to be a pivotal figure in Tall's leadership formation. Tall also spent over seven years in the Sokoto Caliphate, learning from some of the most esteemed Muslim scholars (Robinson, 1985). His time in Futa Toro, Cairo, Mecca, and Medina, all renowned centers of Islamic learning and practice, further expanded his intellectual and spiritual horizons. These experiences afforded Tall a distinct advantage in acquiring Caliphal power, as he was held in high regard across the Arab and Black Muslim worlds for his preparation and erudition.

Similarly, Muhammad Bello's education played a vital role in his rise to Caliphal power. Although he was the son of the Sokoto Caliphate's founder, Usman dan Fodio, his ascension to the throne was not assured. Many believed Abdullahi dan Fodio, Usman's brother, would inherit the leadership (Last, 1967). However, Muhammad Bello strategically positioned himself for leadership. According to his biography, Bello read over 20,000 books in his studies (Sulaiman, 2020). He was raised in the shadow of his father, absorbing knowledge in Qur'anic studies, hadith literature, Islamic jurisprudence, Arabic, philosophy, medicine, and other subjects (Sulaiman, 2020). Bello also engaged in military leadership, commanding half of the Caliphate during his father's reign. Upon Usman's death, despite opposition from Abdullahi's faction, Bello demonstrated his commitment to the Caliphate by aiding Abdullahi in defending his territory. This act led Abdullahi to recognize Bello as the legitimate leader (Last, 1967).

Another prominent Caliph who received an extensive education was Askia Muhammad Bonkana Kiyra (d. 1537) of the Songhay Empire. Askia Muhammad Bonkana Kiyra spent his youth studying near the Sankore Mosque in Timbuktu, a city renowned for its scholarship and vibrant intellectual culture (Gomez, 2018). There, he studied the Islamic sciences under distinguished scholars, contributing to his intellectual preparation for leadership. Though Askia Muhammad was his uncle, Bonkana Kiyra's scholarly demeanor and deep learning earned him the confidence of his family, leading them to choose him as the rightful heir.

Suleyman Bal (d. 1775), a key figure in the Imamate of Futa Toro, also benefited from a solid educational foundation. Bal, who played a critical role in the Islamic revolution that established Islam as the dominant religion in the region, was educated in the Islamic sciences and governance (Robinson, 1975). His leadership not only brought an end to Futa Toro's tributary payments to the Moors but also halted British slave raids in the region. Bal's efforts led to his recognition as the new Almaamy of Futa Toro, despite his initial refusal of the title. Upon his death, Abdul Qadir Kane succeeded him as Almaamy, a figure renowned for his religious scholarship and leadership qualities (Barry, 1988, p.103). Kane's inauguration, during which the entire Qur'an was read, symbolized a new era of Islamic practice in Futa Toro.

Sheikhu Ahmadu (d. 1845) of the Massina Caliphate, another prominent leader, also received exemplary religious training, notably under the mentorship of Sheikh Usman dan Fodio of the Sokoto Caliphate (Adeleye, 1971).

Karamoka Alfa (d. 1751), founder of the Imamate of Futa Djallon, also benefited from a strong educational foundation. Born Alfa Ibrahima Sambegou, this figure is historically recognized as Karamokho Alfa (Sanneh, 2016). The name "Karamokho" reflects his lineage as a scholar and his roots in a well-established clerical tradition (Sanneh, 2016). From a young age, Alfa was immersed in the Islamic sciences and was closely connected to his community's religious practices (Rodney, 1968). He was tutored by some of the most esteemed scholars of West Africa and was known for his spiritual leadership, helping others cultivate inner strength. His deep religious commitment played a significant role in his ability to lead his people effectively. Paul Marty, a French colonial official, described Karamokho Alfa as "the prophet of Israel come to rouse his people from their slumber, to awaken their soporific faith, and to launch them on their grand destiny" (Sanneh, 2016, p. 139).

Although many West African Caliphs did not receive formal Islamic education in their youth, some managed to overcome this gap in their knowledge. Samori Toure, from the Wassoulou Empire, is one such example. Born to a father who practiced traditional religion, Samori became increasingly engaged with Muslims of high caliber after founding his own kingdom. This exposure convinced him of the central importance of Islam, both for his empire and his personal spiritual growth. To further his education, Samori sought guidance from prominent Islamic scholars, particularly Karamokho Sidiki Sherifu, the most respected scholar in Kankan.

Although Samori was already an adult, he was committed to mastering Islamic knowledge and its practical application. Under the tutelage of Karamokho Sidiki Sherifu, he studied the Qur'an, began reading Arabic texts, and achieved a senior level in Qur'anic studies. Over time, Samori began leading prayers in his community (Person, 1979). His followers soon saw themselves as part of a genuine Islamic community. This illustrates that even when formal Islamic education is not received in one's youth, self-directed learning can profoundly shape one's leadership effectiveness.

COURAGE AND MEANS

Beyond education, another consistent factor among those who acquired Caliphal power in West Africa is courage, accompanied by the means to demonstrate it. A significant point made by Machiavelli (2003) regarding prophets is his preference for armed prophets. Machiavelli viewed Moses as an exemplar of what it takes to become a prince, emphasizing his ability to wield force when necessary, as noted in both the Qur'an and the Bible. This attribute of courage is equally crucial among those who attained Caliphal status in West Africa. Much like Machiavelli's advice to seize opportunities and fortune (fortuna), his ideal of bold action aligns with the actions of many Caliphs in this study.

Sheikhu Ahmadu (d. 1845), the founder of the Massina Caliphate (also known as the Caliphate of Hamdalluhi), exemplifies this. Despite being greatly outnumbered, he took the offensive against the formidable Tuareg forces (Nobili, 2020), who were renowned for their cavalry expertise in the arid Sahara Desert. The Tuaregs employed a policy of demanding tribute from towns and trade caravans, often resorting to violence when payments were withheld. Sheikhu Ahmadu,

PERSONALIST RULE: ACQUIRING CALIPHAL POWER

a former student of Usman dan Fodio, received a flag from him to wage jihad, rallying his Fulani kinsmen to fight both the Tuaregs and non-believers (Adeleye, 1971). His courage and determination were critical to his victories, allowing him to establish the Massina Emirate. After Usman dan Fodio's death, Sheikhu Ahmadu declared his independence from the Sokoto Caliphate and proclaimed himself Caliph, marking the birth of the Massina Caliphate. Although the Sokoto Caliphate protested, they were unable to reverse this development. Sheikhu Ahmadu's family would govern the Massina Caliphate for three generations until it was absorbed by the Tukulor Empire under Sheikh al-Hajj Umar Tall (Oloruntimehin, 1972). Sheikhu Ahmadu's rise to power was characterized by both military prowess and bold ambition.

In the late 16th century, Tengella (d. 1512) led a Fulani uprising in Massina (present-day Mali) against the declining Songhay Empire (Rodney, 1970). Although the revolt was suppressed by the Songhay ruler, Tengella led a mass migration of Fulani to the upper Guinea Coast, conquering territories along the way and establishing the Great Fula Empire in Futo Toro and Futa Djallon (Rodney, 1970). Tengella's conquest of these regions, previously under the control of the Wolof and the Songhay Empire, marked the end of Songhay's dominance in the area. Tengella's rise to power is one of the most underappreciated moments in the history of Islam in West Africa. Prior to the establishment of the Great Fula Empire, the Fulani were a subordinate group within the Malian and Songhay Empires. However, the creation of the Great Fula Empire propelled the Fulani to the forefront of West African religious, social, and political movements. Fulani Muslims played a significant role in founding new Islamic states throughout the 17th to 19th centuries (Lovejoy, 2016), and 42% of the founding Caliphs in this study were Fulani.

THE AFRICAN CALIPHS

Sheikh al-Amin al-Kanemi (d. 1837), ruler of the Borno Empire, also exemplified boldness and ambition in his rise to power. When the Mai (king) of Borno faced significant losses due to a Fulani-led uprising, he sought the help of Sheikh al-Amin al-Kanemi, a local cleric and military strategist (Brenner, 1973). Al-Kanemi's military acumen helped quell the revolt and repel foreign invaders, effectively saving the kingdom. In gratitude, the Mai granted al-Kanemi significant control over the armed forces, a decision that would ultimately lead to his ascendancy. Within a short time, al-Kanemi gained the loyalty of the military and other factions, and the Mai became a mere figurehead. Al-Kanemi soon replaced the Mai as the de facto leader of Borno.

Malik Sy's (r. 1690s) leadership in Senegambia is also significant. As the founder of Bundu, the first substantial clerical state in the region (Gomez, 1993), Malik Sy established a state where Muslims could practice their faith free from traditional religious influence. A charismatic and competent military leader (Curtin, 1971), Malik Sy's leadership attracted many immigrants seeking religious freedom. His growing military force enabled him to defend Bundu from raids and expand its territory. Ultimately, Malik Sy declared his independence from the king who had granted him his territory (Curtin, 1971). His ability to build a formidable military and establish a fully Islamic state in a region previously dominated by traditional rulers demonstrates his strategic vision and determination.

The actions of Karamoko Alfa (d. 1751) also illustrate the role of courage and means in acquiring Caliphal power. In Futa Jallon, traditional leaders frequently permitted the capture and enslavement of Muslims, an affront to Islamic law. When a local traditional chief ordered the cessation of public Islamic prayers, the Muslim community rebelled. One cleric, Ibrahima

PERSONALIST RULE: ACQUIRING CALIPHAL POWER

Sori, destroyed the chief's royal drums in protest (Rodney, 1968). Despite disapproving of his cousin's actions, Karamoko Alfa chose not to surrender him. Instead, he led a revolution, organizing a military force to challenge the traditional rulers. After a series of successful skirmishes, a civil war broke out in Futa Jallon. Under Karamoko Alfa's leadership, the Muslims emerged victorious, and the region became known as a Muslim state. The Fulani Muslims of Futa Jallon, previously a tribute-paying class, now became the dominant power, demanding tribute from their former rulers. Karamoko Alfa's decision to act decisively ensured the establishment of a new Muslim state, transforming Futa Jallon's political and religious landscape (Rodney, 1968).

After defeating the ruling aristocracy, Muslim leaders established the Futa Jallon confederation, which comprised nine provinces, with an Almaamy serving as the leader (Rodney, 1968). In this context, the Almaamy is analogous to the Caliph. The term *Almaamy* is derived from the Fulani (Pulaar) interpretation of the Arabic *Al-Imam*, meaning one who leads in prayer. Prior to the revolution, the Fulanis were united under a great leader, Mamadou Sellou, whose charisma, administrative skill, and military force allowed him to control a territory nearly as large as the Futa Jallon itself (Rodney, 1968). Although Mamadou Sellou seemed the logical choice to become the ruling Almaamy after the revolution, the leaders of the provinces chose Karamoko Alfa instead. This decision marked a significant shift in West African leadership, as Karamoko Alfa was selected not for his military prowess or inheritance, but for his religious piety and learning (Barry, 1988). As Machiavelli (2003) observed, armed prophets must not only possess military strength but also exude religious piety, which underpins their leadership. While Mamadou Sellou was formidable in battle, Karamoko Alfa excelled in religious devotion and could support his authority with both spiritual and military power.

A similar figure, Sheikh Usman dan Fodio (d. 1817), exemplifies the fusion of religious authority and military success. As the founder of the Sokoto Caliphate, the largest and most influential Islamic polity in West Africa until the colonial period, his leadership grew following the defeat of the Tuareg regime during the dry season of 1805-06 (Lovejoy, 2016; Last, 1967, p. 36). The Tuareg regime had long manipulated Hausa rulers, fostering internal conflict and exploiting their subjects. After Sokoto's victory, Sheikh Usman dan Fodio sent letters to Muslim leaders in different Hausa kingdoms, such as Daura, Kano, Katsina, and Zamfara, urging them to pledge allegiance to him in accordance with the Qur'an and the Sunnah of Prophet Muhammad (Last, 1967). By requesting *bay'a* (the pledge of allegiance), Sheikh Usman dan Fodio demonstrated both his past military successes and his capacity to enforce his authority when necessary. From this point, his leadership extended beyond his immediate followers to encompass several Hausa states, and he garnered the loyalty of other Muslims seeking reform. Given the Sheikh's efforts, his Islamic polity expanded "from the city-state of Gobir, into a West African super-state" (Sulaiman, 1987, p. 1).

It is important to note that although Sheikh Usman dan Fodio did not initially seek regime change, the oppressive actions of the ruling powers compelled him to do so. Their harsh treatment of devout Muslims and the heavy taxes imposed on the pastoralist Fulanis led Sheikh Usman dan Fodio and his followers to organize as a fighting force (Sulaiman, 2009). Their subsequent victories expanded Sheikh Usman dan Fodio's influence as Muslims from various regions sought his help to overthrow repressive rulers (Adeleye, 1971). Many reformers joined his cause, carrying the banner of his jihad, which not

PERSONALIST RULE: ACQUIRING CALIPHAL POWER

only rallied Muslims but also convinced reluctant populations that the revolution was divinely inspired.

Another notable figure is Ma Ba Diakhu (d. 1867), ruler of Rip, who combined political acumen, military prowess, and an exceptional eye for talent. During his Islamic revolution to liberate Muslims from secular rulers who enslaved them, Ma Ba Diakhu welcomed two prominent royals into his cause: Lat Dior (d. 1886), the former king of Kayoor fleeing the French, and Albuuri Ndjay (d. 1901), who would later rule Jolof (Robinson, 1991). The condition for their participation in Ma Ba Diakhu's revolution was their conversion to Islam, which both accepted (Robinson, 1991).

Similarly, Sunni Ali (d. 1492) provides another example of a leader who overcame significant challenges to establish authority. Although Sunni Ali ascended the throne of Songhay after his father's death, he was not the intended heir. As Gomez (2018) cites from Al-Maghili, "with his father's death, Ali sought power and rose up against Songhay, fighting them until he overcame them and gained dominion over them, as his father and other sultans of Songhay had done before him" (p. 184). Sunni Ali founded the Songhay Empire through military conquest, and under his leadership, Songhay expanded, incorporating key Islamic centers such as Timbuktu. While not the most devout Caliph, Sunni Ali's military achievements and expansion of Islam were unparalleled in this context.

Muhammad Kanta's (d. 1561) rise to power in Kebbi also exemplifies the use of military strength and bold action to claim leadership. Muhammad Kanta, a Hausa general in the Songhay Empire, claimed Kebbi's independence after a successful campaign against the Tuaregs in Agadez. Upon learning that he and his men would not receive their fair share of the spoils, he declared Kebbi independent. Despite attempts by Songhay forces to reclaim the province, Muhammad Kanta's strategic brilliance and natural defenses of Kebbi led to their repeated defeats. He became the first Sarkin (king) of Kebbi and its first Caliph (Gomez, 2018).

Not every factor leading to the acquisition of Caliphal authority is palatable to the more sensitive individual. In fact, Machiavelli (2003) famously remarked that if one desires leaders to be saints, they should look to the church. As the renowned political philosopher notes, politics is a messy business, and those who engage in it must be prepared to get their hands dirty. However, Machiavelli also argues that while one's hands may be sullied, a good prince must know how to make them appear clean and innocent. A well-known method of acquiring power is through bribery. Askia Ismail (d. 1539) of the Songhay Empire, for example, orchestrated a successful coup by leveraging gold. Specifically, he used a trove of gold entrusted to a slave loyal to his father to buy the allegiance of several key officials, thereby securing his position on the throne (Gomez, 2018).

Askia Musa (d. 1531), the son of the revered Askia Muhammad, was infuriated when his father appointed a relatively unknown figure as governor of a prestigious province, likely signaling his intentions to name him successor. After inquiring into the matter, Musa discovered that the decision had been influenced by his father's most trusted (and overly ambitious) advisors. Moreover, Musa learned that his father had been blind for some time. Upon this revelation, Musa and his followers deposed the Askia and allowed him a peaceful retirement. Musa then ascended to the title of Askia Musa, becoming one of the wealthiest individuals in the world at the time. Although his father was granted a peaceful retirement, Musa and his followers killed between 30 and 40 of his brothers, cousins, and other kinsmen to solidify his claim to the throne. Prior to seizing power, Musa also killed his uncle. It was not

PERSONALIST RULE: ACQUIRING CALIPHAL POWER

long before Askia Musa was assassinated by a coalition of his remaining brothers, led by Mohammad Benkan and Alu Way. After a two-day revolt, Alu Way mortally wounded Askia Musa, ending his tumultuous and bloody two-year reign. Following Musa's death, Mohammad Benkan assumed the title of Askia.

Bubu Malik Sy (d. 1727), son of the founder of Bundu, is included here because, despite his father's founding of the state, he was not next in the line of succession. Malik Sy, the founder, had an agreement with two other prominent groups in Bundu, under which the senior member of the three groups was to become the supreme leader (Gomez, 1987). Bubu Malik Sy's junior status in relation to the other groups' senior members disqualified him from succeeding his father. However, he seized power by leveraging his strength in manpower and receiving support from neighboring Futa Jallon (Gomez, 1987). After Bubu Malik Sy's reign, Bundu experienced a brief interregnum during which no clear leader emerged. Several years later, Bubu Malik Sy's son, Maka Jiba, reclaimed the title for his family after a short-armed struggle with rival notables.

When Amadi Gai (d. 1786) of Bundu was passed over for the Almaamate, he was furious. He ordered his slave to assassinate the attending village head, causing the conference to descend into chaos. In the aftermath, his branch of the royal family elected him as Almaamy (Gomez, 1994). To secure his position, Amadi Gai negotiated with non-Muslim kingdoms and forced the other claimant to the throne into exile. Similarly, Ibrahim Kura (c. 1786) became Shehu of Borno by bribing the royal riflemen to support his claim to the throne over his more popular uncle (Brenner, 1973). With the backing of this elite military group, Ibrahim Kura coerced the electors and religious leaders into selecting him as Shehu, under threat of violence. They ultimately complied, and Ibrahim Kura was duly installed (Brenner, 1973). These examples underscore the critical importance of exercising strategic control over the armed forces.

SPIRITUAL AUTHORITY

Most of the African Caliphs in this study, though not all, possessed significant spiritual authority. As indicated in Table 3, spiritual authority was a defining characteristic of all initiators of Islam. Among these initiators, 43% acquired their authority as revolutionaries. The level of spiritual authority required to lead a successful revolution must be immense, as such leaders must overcome the major challenge of collective action (Olsen, 1965). In revolutionary movements, people must be inspired to such an extent that they are willing to risk their lives (and often their families' lives) to achieve the leader's vision. To gain this trust and dedication, leaders must effectively translate their spiritual authority into action.

Spiritual authority is often acquired through a life of learning, devotion, and piety. However, political leaders may also acquire it through conversion and subsequent efforts to spread the faith within their realm. Several leaders in this study exemplify this transformation, having embraced Islam and worked diligently to promote its mission.

One notable example is Mai Umme (r. 1085–1097), the first Caliph of Bornu. As the 12th Mai of the Sefuwa dynasty, his conversion to Islam in the 11th century marked his rise as the dynasty's first Caliph. Mai Umme is celebrated in the chronicles of Kanem-Bornu for his role in Islamizing the region. He made two pilgrimages to Mecca and died in Egypt while preparing for a third. Performing the Hajj was a significant event for West African Muslims in the precolonial period, conferring both baraka and prestige within their Islamic communities.

PERSONALIST RULE: ACQUIRING CALIPHAL POWER

Haji I (d. 1385), the first Muslim Caliph of Kano, provides another example of spiritual authority gained through conversion. He embraced Islam early in his reign as Sarkin of Kano, largely due to the efforts of Muslim scholars and traders from the Malian Empire (Palmer, 1908). Under his leadership, Islam became the dominant religion of Kano, which later became a prominent center of Islamic learning in West Africa. Haji I's piety and baraka were legendary among the Hausa. It is said that during a battle with non-Muslim forces for control of Kano, Haji I prayed to Allah for victory. Upon completing his prayer, his chief opponent was struck blind, and following further prayers, additional enemies suffered the same fate, leading to their surrender (Palmer, 1908).

Another example is Mamadu Juhe, the leader of the Hubbu Confederation in the Senegambia region. Known for his piety and intellectual contributions, Mamadu Juhe was highly respected, particularly for his role in religious education among the region's aristocracy (Barry, 1998). As the Transatlantic Slave Trade ravaged the region, economic and social instability escalated. Rulers imposed heavy taxes, which many saw as unjust and contrary to Islamic principles. In response to the growing social unrest and the greed associated with the slave trade, Mamadu Juhe and his followers established a separate Islamic state in Futa Jallon, providing protection from the ravages of the trade (Greene, 2015). The state, which attracted traders, runaway slaves, and others seeking a more egalitarian form of Islam, endured for over 30 years before being defeated by the forces of Samori Toure.

Za-kassi, the first Muslim Caliph of Songhay, offers another illustration of spiritual authority. As the fifteenth monarch of the Za dynasty, he converted to Islam voluntarily around A.H. 400 (A.D. 1009-1010). There are no specific accounts of the influences behind his conversion (Arnold, 1913).

Likewise, King Kunburu of Jenne, who converted to Islam around 1200 A.D., is noted for leading his people in their conversion. His strong embrace of Islam inspired the voluntary conversion of all the city's inhabitants (Arnold, 1913). Today, Jenne is home to the renowned Great Mosque, which sits atop the ruins of Kunburu's former palace. It is said that Kunburu demolished his palace to construct the mosque on its foundation.

CONCLUSION

This chapter explores several African Caliphs who gained political authority through their own ambition and determination. Their vision and confidence in their abilities enabled them to acquire power. Additionally, the chapter introduces the founders of Islamic states during West Africa's Classical Islamic period. Unlike others who maneuvered within existing systems by replacing incumbents, these founders not only established their own polities but also introduced entirely new systems of social practice. For example, Malik Sy's Bundu became a refuge for Muslims, welcoming only those who renounced their traditional lifestyles and embraced the precepts of Islam.

The diverse methods by which African Caliphs acquired power are striking. I categorize these methods into six types: conversion, revolution, coup, secession, inheritance, and election. Revolution was the most common means of gaining Caliphal authority during West Africa's Classical Islamic period. This is understable, given the turmoil caused by the Transatlantic Slave Trade, which disrupted established social orders and created widespread unrest. As Barry (1998) argues, the slave trade both destabilized regional hierarchies and prompted people to either exploit the trade's benefits or escape its devastations.

While recent coups in West Africa since 2017 have been seen by some as a unique phenomenon or a legacy of colonialism, historical analysis reveals that political coups have been a consistent feature of West African politics since at least the 11th century. Alongside these revolutions, many conversions to Islam took place. Some of these conversions were opportunistic, aimed at gaining access to the benefits of trade and political power associated with Islam. However, others were motivated by sincere religious devotion, as leaders sought to improve their societies and themselves by adopting Islam. This conversion enabled them to integrate into a vast international network of traders, scholars, and religious practitioners.

REFERENCES

Adeleye, R. A. (1971). *Power and diplomacy in northern Nigeria, 1804–1906: The Sokoto Caliphate and its enemies.* London.

Arnold, T. W. (1913). *The preaching of Islam: A history of the propagation of the Muslim faith.* New York: C. Scribner's Sons.

Barry, B. (1998). *Senegambia and the Atlantic slave trade.* Cambridge University Press: United Kingdom.

Brenner, L. (1973). *The Shehus of Kukawa: A history of the Al-Kanemi dynasty of Bornu.* Clarendon Press: Oxford.

Colvin, L. G. (1974). Islam and the state of Kajoor: A case of successful resistance to jihad. *The Journal of African History, 15*(4), 587–606.

Curtin, P. (1971). Jihad in West Africa: Early phases and inter-relations in Mauritania and Senegal. *The Journal of African History, 12*(1), 11–24.

Gomez, M. A. (2018). *African dominion: A new history of empire in early and medieval West Africa.* Princeton University Press.

Gomez, M. (1987). Bundu in the eighteenth century. *The International Journal of African Historical Studies, 20*(1), 61–73.

Gomez, M. (1993). *Pragmatism in the age of jihad: The precolonial state of Bundu*. Cambridge University Press.

Greene, S. E. (2015). Minority voices: Abolitionism in West Africa. *Slavery & Abolition, 36*(4), 642–661.

Last, M. (1967). *The Sokoto Caliphate*. London: Longmans, Green, and Co. Ltd.

Levtzion, N. (1980). *Ancient Ghana and Mali*. London: Africana Publishing Company.

Lovejoy, P. E. (2016). *Jihād in West Africa during the age of revolutions* (1st ed.). Ohio University Press.

Machiavelli, N., & Bull, G. (2003). *The prince*. Penguin Classics.

Nobili, M. (2020). Sultan, caliph, and the renewer of the faith: Aḥmad Lobbo, the *Tārīkh al-fattāsh* and the making of an Islamic state in West Africa. *African Studies*. Cambridge University Press.

Oloruntimehin, B. O. (1972). *The Segu Tukulor Empire*. New York: Humanities Press.

Olson, M. (1965). *The logic of collective action: Public goods and the theory of groups*. Harvard University Press.

Palmer, H. R. (Ed.). (1908). *The Kano Chronicle. Journal of the Royal Anthropological Institute of Great Britain and Ireland, 38*, 58–98.

Person, Y. (1979). *Samori and Islam*. In J. Willis. (Ed.), *Studies in West African Islamic History: The Cultivators of Islam* (pp. 259–277). Routledge.

Robinson, D. (1991). Beyond resistance and collaboration: Amadu Bamba and the Murids of Senegal. *Journal of Religion in Africa, 21*(2), 149–171.

Robinson, D. (1985). *The holy war of Umar Tal: The Western Sudan in the mid-nineteenth century*. Oxford: Clarendon Press.

Robinson, D. (1975). The Islamic revolution of Futa Toro. *The International Journal of African Historical Studies, 8*(2), 185–221.

Rodney, W. (1970). *A history of the Upper Guinea Coast: 1545–1800*. New York: Monthly Review Press.

Rodney, W. (1968). Jihad and social revolution in Futa Djalon in the eighteenth century. *Journal of the Historical Society of Nigeria, 4*(2), 269–284.

Sulaiman, I. (2009). *The African Caliphate: The life, works & teachings of Shaykh Usman Dan Fodio (1754–1817)*. London: The Diwan Press Ltd.

Sulaiman, I. (2020). *The African Caliphate 2: Ideals, policies and operation of the Sokoto Caliphate*. London: The Diwan Press Ltd.

Willis, J. (1989). *In the path of Allah: The passion of Al-Hajj Umar: An essay into the nature of charisma in Islam*. 2 Park Square, Milton Park, Abingdon, Oxon: Frank Cass & Co. Ltd.

CHAPTER 5

MAINTAINING CALIPHAL POWER

Statute of Askia al-Hajj Muhammad of the Songhay Empire in present-day Mali

Conrad, David C. (2005). *Great Empires of the Past: Empires of Medieval West Africa*. Chelsea House, pg.110

CHAPTER 5

PERSONALIST RULE: MAINTAINING CALIPHAL POWER

This chapter contributes to the study of African political leadership by offering valuable insights into the strategic and multifaceted methods employed by West African Caliphs to maintain power. It explores factors that contributed to the ability of Caliphs to remain on the throne. As the previous chapter demonstrates, acquiring caliphal authority generally requires boldness, bravery, and piety. However, as the saying goes, while winning control of government is one thing, governing is quite another. In this context, although it takes certain skills to acquire caliphal authority, maintaining that authority in the face of diverse threats demands an entirely different set of capabilities. This chapter identifies several factors observed to aid Caliphs in sustaining power. These factors do not guarantee perpetual rule, but collectively, they highlight commonalities that have contributed to the prolonged reign of Caliphs across time and space in Islamic West Africa.

The factors identified as assisting African Caliphs in maintaining power during the Classical Islamic period include: (a) outward displays of faith, piety, and religious symbolism (including strict adherence to prayers), (b) magnanimity (including charisma and confidence), (c) sound organization, and (d) strategic thinking. Many of these factors work synergistically and are not mutually exclusive. Examples of each are provided to isolate their effects and illustrate their utility. Maintaining power is a central aspect of ruling within a personalist political system, and it is a constant concern for African Caliphs.

Bueno de Mesquita et al.'s (1999) concept of selectorate theory offers insights into maintaining political power, which is highly relevant to understanding African Caliphs during West Africa's Classical Islamic period. However, while selectorate theory is useful for analyzing contemporary states and polities, it provides limited insights when applied to the political systems of the Classical Islamic period in West Africa.

Selectorate theory posits that maintaining political power is the singular concern of rulers, and everything leaders do is aimed at preserving that power. In a personalist system, however, there are notable differences. For example, selectorate theory advises keeping subjects weak and dependent to ensure their submission, even if they are dissatisfied. In contrast, personalist rule depends on the specific context. The ultimate goal of many (though not all) personalist rulers during the Classical Islamic period was to establish and maintain Islam. The title of Caliph was merely a means to advance this goal. For example, after Shehu Usman dan Fodio became Caliph of the Sokoto Empire, he delegated control of the empire to his son and brother while he focused on spiritual matters (Sulaiman, 2020). By distributing administrative responsibilities rather than consolidating power, Shehu Usman dan Fodio's actions demonstrate the need to revise certain assumptions in selectorate theory to better account for the political practices of African Caliphs.

Another divergence from selectorate theory is its view on the futility of disenfranchised citizens. Islam does not recognize the concept of disenfranchised citizens, and states that model themselves on the Quran and Sunnah similarly do not subscribe to this idea. During the Classical Islamic period in West Africa, people often migrated across state boundaries for various reasons. For instance, according to Willis (1989), many warriors and citizens of al-Hajj Umar Tall's Tukulor Empire, with its capital at Segu (present-day Mali), came from throughout the Western Sahel and the Senegambian region (present-day Senegal, Gambia, Guinea, Mauritania, and Guinea-Bissau). As the demand for soldiers, farmers, and other forms of manpower grew during this period, African Caliphs could ill afford to overlook any citizen or potential citizen. When African Caliphs spoke or acted, Muslims from across the region took notice. Their actions often inspired Muslims from distant areas to migrate and join the cause. This can be seen with figures such as Shehu Usman dan Fodio (Sulaiman, 2009), al-Hajj Umar Tall (Willis, 1989), and Sheikh Ahmadu Lobbo (Nobili, 2020). These leaders intentionally addressed an audience far beyond their immediate territories, calling Muslims everywhere to join their movements. Many Muslims responded affirmatively to these calls. In the remainder of this chapter, I will explore several key factors observed to help African Caliphs maintain their hold on power from the perspective of personalist rule.

OUTWARD DISPLAYS OF FAITH, PIETY, AND RELIGIOUS SYMBOLISM

Faith and piety are fundamental aspects of religion, demonstrating one's commitment, seriousness, and devotion to its requirements. For Muslim leaders in West Africa during the Classical Islamic period, public displays of faith and piety were essential for maintaining the allegiance of the most devout followers and, consequently, securing political power. These displays also helped to thwart internal challenges for power from less religious contenders. As Islam increasingly spread throughout West Africa, the Muslim elite and faithful emerged as a crucial power bloc for state rulers. Consequently, many charismatic religious leaders gained popularity among the Muslim elite, forming strong alliances with them. From the 11th to the 19th centuries, many non-Islamic leaders were replaced by Muslim rulers. In many cases, the qualities of fairness or equity of non-Muslim leaders were irrelevant; the mere fact that they were not Muslim rendered their rule illegitimate in the eyes of the faithful.

In an era and region where Islam was spreading rapidly, it became necessary not only to possess faith and piety but also to visibly demonstrate these qualities. As will be discussed, many Caliphs strategically used religious symbolism during their reigns. One of the most powerful tools in the arsenal of West African Caliphs was the ability to leverage symbolism and historical precedence. Symbols play a crucial role in societies, as they can help unite communities by linking institutions and beliefs with emotions and normative behaviors. According to Theiler (2017), symbols influence preferences, identities, and behavior. In this context, Caliphs harnessed the religious fervor of the people by invoking important Islamic themes and ideas in their decision-making. The use of symbols and other public displays of faith and piety became key strategies for Caliphs in West Africa to maintain political power.

Abdul Qadir Khan (d.1806), in his efforts to abolish the slave trade in the Senegambian region and protect Muslims from enslavement, blocked French slave ships from entering his jurisdiction (Ware, 2013). If he encountered any Africans in chains, he freed those who could recite even a single phrase from the Qur'an (Ware, 2013). As a result, even non-Muslims were freed if they could demonstrate knowledge of Islam's holy text. This display of faith and mercy garnered him a large

PERSONALIST RULE: MAINTAINING CALIPHAL POWER

following, extending beyond Muslim communities. As the Almaamy of the newly established and powerful Futa Toro Imamate, Abdul Qadir Khan also oversaw the construction of mosques in each village within his domain (Robinson, 1973). Each mosque was staffed with a learned Imam to encourage religious observance, and the Almaamy promoted religious education in every village. Futa Toro became one of the foremost centers of Islamic learning in Africa, rivaling Timbuktu and Jenne in present-day Mali. This emphasis on learning, scholarship, and Islamic practice solidified a distinct Muslim identity in the region, elevating the Almaamy's prestige and establishing him as one of the most revered figures in political life. Abdul Qadir Khan cultivated a devoted following, and his reputation as a man of God was so strong that even after being captured in battle, his captor allowed him to return home out of respect for his piety.

On one stormy and muddy evening, Askia Ishaq of the Songhay Empire (d.1549) attended communal prayer at the mosque, accompanied by the Imam and the muaddhin (the person who calls the faithful to prayer). The latter two assumed that no one else would brave the storm, especially not the Askia, who they presumed would remain in the warmth of his royal bed. As they prepared to begin prayer, however, Askia Ishaq surprised them by appearing, demonstrating his personal commitment to the faith (Gomez, 2018). This episode became legendary and highlighted Askia Ishaq's devotion, strengthening his image as a pious and revered leader. Similarly, another Askia, Askia Muhammad (d. 1538) of the Songhay Empire, also illustrates the strategic importance of demonstrating piety and faith to his people. An episode from Gomez's (2018) account of the *Tarikh al-Fattash* is particularly illustrative:

> "Then he [the *askia*] said to him [Maḥmūd] after the completion of the greetings and salutations, "I sent to you my envoys

bearing my concerns—did you carry out my order in Timbuktu? No! Rather, you sent back my messengers and forbid them from making my concerns evident. Did not the Mali-*koi* rule Timbuktu?" The *shaykh* [Maḥmūd] replied, "Without question, he ruled it." He [the *askia*] continued, "In those days, was there not a *qāḍī* in Timbuktu?" He [Maḥmūd] said, "There certainly was." He [the *askia*] said, "Are you greater than that *qāḍī*, or is he greater than you?" He answered, "No doubt, he is greater than me, and more illustrious." Then the *askia* said, "Did his [the Mali-*koi*'s] *qāḍī* prevent him from acting freely in Timbuktu?" He [Maḥmūd] replied, "No, he did not prevent him." Then the *askia* said, "Were not the Tuareg the rulers (*sulṭāns*) of Timbuktu?" And he replied, "They certainly were." He [the *askia*] continued, "Was there not a *qāḍī* in it in those days?" He answered, "Certainly it was so." The *askia* said, "Are you greater than that *qāḍī*, or is he greater than you?" The *shaykh* replied, "Surely he is greater than me and more illustrious." Then he [the *askia*] said to him, "Did not Chi [Sunni 'Alī] rule Timbuktu?" The *shaykh* said, "He surely did." He [the *askia*] continued, "In those days, was there not a *qāḍī* in it?" He replied, "There was." Then he [the *askia*] said, "He feared God more than you, or do you fear [God] more than he, and are you more illustrious?" He replied, "Without question, he was more God-fearing than I, and more illustrious." Then he [the *askia*] said, "Did these *qāḍīs* prevent these rulers from acting freely in Timbuktu, or were they able to do in the city whatever they wanted regarding matters of government and taxation?" Then he [Maḥmūd] answered, "They did not place an obstacle between them and their desires." Then he [the *askia*] said, "Then why do *you* [emphasis added] prohibit me [from doing the same], and restrain my hand and reject my messengers whom I sent to carry out my wishes; and [why did you] beat them and order their expulsion from the land [the city]? What's wrong with you? What's going on here? How do you explain this?!" (Gomez, 2018, p. 269 | TF, 60–61/115–17.)

In this exchange, the Askia and a prominent Islamic *qadi* (judge) disagreed over the former's imposition of taxes inconsistent with *sharia*. As an Islamic jurist and scholar, the qadi believed it was his duty not only to inform the Askia of his obligation to avoid reintroducing traditional systems of taxation but also to confront him on the matter if necessary. According to Gomez (2018), the *qadi* felt responsible for ensuring the Muslim community's alignment with Islamic law and protecting the commercial interests of the local population. The *qadi* reminded the Askia of his earlier request for guidance throughout his reign to help him avoid hellfire in the Hereafter. Given the *qadi*'s stature and expertise, the Askia ultimately yielded to his determination. This decision enhanced the Askia's reputation as a man of faith, piety, and commitment to Islamic law.

In a notable encounter with the people of Jenne, Askia Ishaq Ber I of the Songhay Empire (d. 1549) demonstrated his ability to leverage public displays of religious adherence for political gain. Askia Ishaq Ber I, also known as Ishaq Kadibini (the Black Stone), was described as regal, learned, and majestic. However, people from several of Songhay's leading towns also portrayed him as ruthless and exploitative, extracting harsh taxes from his subjects. To address grievances and stop the actions of those damaging the Muslim community in Jenne, Askia Ishaq Ber I convened the people of the town. During this meeting, a man named Mahmud Baghayughu spoke up, prompting the following scene:

> "Are you sincere in what you're saying, oh Isḥāq?" "By God, I am in earnest," the *askia* responded. "If we make known this tyrant to you, what will you do to him?" [The *askia* replied to the *faqīh*], "I will give him what he deserves, whether it is death, or a beating, or imprisonment, or exile, or restoring whatever property he destroyed, making him pay a fine." The *faqīh* Maḥmūd Baghayughu, may God be pleased with him, replied, "We know of no one here more tyrannical than *you* [emphasis added], as you are the father of and reason for all that is unjust, for no one here illegally seizes [wealth] by force except you, by

your authority and on your orders. If you want to kill the tyrant, begin with yourself, and be quick about it! This wealth that you have taken from here to enrich yourself, is it [really] yours? Do you have slaves here who cultivate the soil for you, or assets that generate wealth for you?" (Gomez, 2018, p. 274).

Rather than immediately executing Baghayughu for such audacity, Askia Ishaq Ber I is said to have cried and begged for forgiveness publicly. Far from appearing weak due to his tears, the Askia appeared pious and repentant. Rather than resenting the Askia for his previous abuses, the people expressed contempt for Baghayughu for speaking so disrespectfully to the Sultan. The crowd, along with the Askia's security, was ready to attack Baghayughu, but the intervention of the Askia prevented such an action. By demonstrating repentance before his subjects, the Askia won their hearts and affections. In African religious contexts, piety is not attributed merely to scholarly proficiency but to noble deeds and virtuous actions. By submitting to the admonitions of the ulama, the Sultan affirmed his role as both the temporal and spiritual leader of West Africa.

Another example of a successful display of Caliphal piety, which further extended the ruler's legacy, involves a Hausa slave returning from Hajj (the Islamic pilgrimage). According to Gomez (2018), upon the return of those who had fulfilled the sacred rites of Hajj, Askia Dawud (d. 1582) kissed the hands of the returning entourage, as was customary. When he reached the Hausa slave, however, a member of the group interrupted the act. This individual believed the Askia should not defile his royal lips by kissing the hands of someone so lowly. Offended by the Hausa slave's audacity, the member suggested that the slave's hands be amputated. In his confusion, Askia Dawud turned to his legal advisor for guidance. The advisor responded as follows:

PERSONALIST RULE: MAINTAINING CALIPHAL POWER

> How is it not lawful to cut off the hand of someone who stood at Arafat, who circumambulated the Ka'ba, who placed that hand on the Black Stone, and then touched the Yemeni Corner (rukn al-yamānī), and with that hand participated in the two stonings [at Mina], then visited the Messenger of God [in Medina] (may God bless him and grant him peace) and placed this hand on the chair (maq'ad) of the Messenger of God's noble pulpit (may God bless him and grant him peace), and then entered the garden (al-rawḍa al-sharīfa) [in the Prophet's mosque, between the pulpit and the room where he is buried], and placed this hand on the grate that surrounds [the Prophet's tomb], and then placed it on the tombs of Abū Bakr and 'Umar (may God be pleased with them). But not satisfied with all these privileges and advantages and commendable acts, [he] came to you to place this hand in yours, by so doing he might achieve the most modest and fleeting of earthly goals (Gomez, 2018, p. 348).

Thus moved, Askia Dawud not only pardons the Hausa slave but also frees him from bondage permanently. He grants freedom to hundreds of members of the Hausa slave's family and exempts them from taxes. Additionally, he imprisons the individual who had originally raised objections (Gomez, 2018). These actions demonstrate the high regard and value the pious Caliph places on those who successfully complete the sacred rites of the Islamic Hajj. This episode is recorded in both oral traditions and the historical chronicles of Islamic West Africa.

Askia Muhammad used his Hajj as a symbolic act to affirm and strengthen his religious legitimacy as the ruler of the Songhay Empire (Gomez, 2018). He employed sacred Islamic symbolism from the pilgrimage to reinforce his position as both a religious and political leader. During his journey, he met revered Islamic figures such as Al-Maghili (1425–1505) and Al-Suyuti (1445–1505), as well as the Abbasid Caliph in Egypt, who recognized him as the Caliph of West Africa (Gomez, 2018). While Askia Muhammad's Hajj may be less famous than that of

Mansa Musa, he donated more wealth to the holy cities than his predecessor. His pilgrimage helped to solidify his legacy, placing it on par with that of Mansa Musa of Mali. Furthermore, because Askia Muhammad had seized power through a coup and was not in the royal line of succession, the Hajj reinforced his religious standing among Muslims in his kingdom. If his rule had been questioned prior to this, his legitimacy was affirmed through the success of his pilgrimage to the Islamic holy sites.

Askia Musa of the Songhay Empire (d. 1531) chose the significant Islamic occasion of Eid al-Adha to seize power from his father (Gomez, 2018). Just before his father was to lead the congregation for the day's observances, Musa and some of his brothers approached him and demanded that he transfer power to Musa. They vowed not to leave until he was named Askia. Seeing no alternative, the father relented, and Musa assumed leadership, leading the people in the Eid al-Adha service (Gomez, 2018). In Islam, Eid al-Adha is the Feast of Sacrifice. Rather than engage in a violent battle for power, Askia Muhammad made the sacrificial gesture of relinquishing the throne to his son. This act symbolized the legitimacy of the transfer of power. Although Musa would later face challenges from other family members, this moment during Eid al-Adha provided him with a brief period of stability.

When Askia Muhammad Bonkana Kirya (d. 1537) learned that the leader of a particular province had killed and beheaded his rebellious brother, Alu Way, he expressed gratitude to the leader, only to have him executed (Gomez, 2018). This was to assert that only royalty may shed the blood of royalty. Failing to address this breach of protocol would have undermined the respect for the Caliphal bloodline. The message was clear: only royalty has the right to take the life of royalty.

Sheikhu Amadu Lobbo (d. 1845) of the Massina Caliphate (also known as the Hamdullahi Caliphate) declared himself the twelfth Imam and the restorer of the faith as described in early Islam (Nobili, 2020). By making this claim and ensuring its inclusion in the religious texts and historical records of West Africa, he legitimized his rule and justified his efforts to spread Islam. This declaration positioned him alongside other significant religious figures, presenting him as divinely chosen by God. This was a strategic move. After leading a successful jihad under the banner of Sheikh Usman dan Fodio's revolutionary movement, Sheikhu Amadu Lobbo broke away from Sokoto (following Usman dan Fodio's death) and claimed the newly conquered territory as his own. To solidify his authority among his new subjects and the former allies he had fought alongside, he focused on controlling religious literature and means of written communication to promote himself as the fulfillment of previous prophecies. His efforts were successful, and his family ruled the Massina Caliphate for three centuries.

As Samori Touré (d. 1898) of the Wassoulou Empire grew deeper in his Islamic faith, he began publicly embracing its practices, despite the continued adherence of many in his kingdom to traditional religions. He distanced himself from traditional celebrations, even though his father and other family members publicly reprimanded him for abandoning their ancestral beliefs (Person, 1979). During the holy month of Ramadan, he openly gave gifts to his subordinates and adopted the religious title of *Almaamy* to signal his alignment with the divine realm rather than the material world (Person, 1979).

STRICT ADHERENCE TO PRAYERS

Several instances of public displays of prayer are notable in this context. Scholars, such as Fisher (1971), have extensively discussed the significance of prayer in West Africa. To summarize, adherence to the Islamic command to pray at prescribed times offered leaders a strategic advantage by appealing to the masses, especially during times of national crisis, war, or public celebration. For example, Al-Kanemi of the Kanem-Bornu Empire (d. 1837) prayed with his disciples for seven days before leading a military campaign to defend Bornu (Fisher, 1971). The prayers proved effective, and Al-Kanemi's forces successfully defeated their enemies. Similarly, Al-Hajj Umar offered prayers for his troops before each military campaign, ensuring that all of his soldiers participated (Fisher, 1971). Rather than invoking a traditional war cry, Sheikh Umar Tall and his troops chanted the Tijaniyya dhikr before entering battle (Fisher, 1971).

Muhammad Bello, Amir al-Muminim of the Sokoto Caliphate (d. 1837), also demonstrated devotion to prayer during military campaigns. On one occasion, he prayed before giving the order to attack a rebellious province. While waiting for water to perform his ablutions, the head of the rebel leader was presented to him. This event further underscored the link between prayer and success. In another instance, Bello and his forces, preparing to attack the Hausa state of Gobir, spent hours in prayer before proceeding with the attack, despite being ready by 4 a.m. (Fisher, 1971).

Mai Idriss Alooma (d. 1603) of the Borno Empire placed significant emphasis on his religious devotions and prayer. During military campaigns, both he and his soldiers observed the fast of Ramadan and maintained the five daily prayers (A.W., 1927). Despite the physical strain of battle, compounded by fatigue from hunger and thirst due to fasting, they exhibited remarkable mental resilience and unwavering devotion to their faith. As Mai Alooma's reputation for moral discipline and integrity spread, it served as a powerful motivator, encouraging others to embrace the faith.

PERSONALIST RULE: MAINTAINING CALIPHAL POWER

The Muslim rulers of Senegambia were equally devoted to their ritual prayers. For instance, Ma Ba Diakhou of Jolof (d. 1867) prayed with his men before successfully attacking and capturing Jolof (Charles, 1977). Similarly, Sheikh Amadu Ba, another ruler of Jolof, led his troops in chanting Tijaniyya verses before going into battle (Charles, 1977).

CONFIDENCE

A king must exhibit regal authority, and a Caliph must possess the confidence to ensure that no other prince considers themselves superior. For example, Mansa Musa (d. 1337) refused to perform the customary prostration before the Sultan of Egypt while en route to the Hajj. Although such prostrations were customary among other rulers in the region, Mansa Musa, as the Caliph of West Africa and leader of the Land of the Blacks, considered them beneath him (Gomez, 2018). This act of defiance reinforced his reputation as the foremost Islamic leader in Muslim West Africa. He declared that he would bow only to Allah, and his refusal to prostrate before mere mortals became legendary even among Muslims in the Arabian Peninsula.

Another example of Caliphal confidence is found in the case of Musa (d. 1531), the son of Askia al-Hajj Muhammad and future Askia. When the governorship of Benga province became vacant, Askia al-Hajj Muhammad appointed his son Balla to the position, bypassing some of his older sons, who became angered and plotted to kill him. However, when confronted by Balla and his entourage, the older brothers dismounted and performed the customary prostrations to acknowledge Balla's authority. Only one brother, Musa, refused to dismount. Although this defiance was a violation of protocol, none of Balla's commanders dared challenge Musa due to his reputation as a courageous and formidable leader (Gomez, 2018, p. 309). When Musa later deposed his father, no one initially dared to oppose him due to his esteemed reputation.

A similar display of confidence occurred when Almaamy Abdul Qadir Kane (d. 1806) learned that Sega of Bundu was pillaging Muslim villages and selling their inhabitants into slavery. In response, Abdul Qadir Kane sent a letter demanding an immediate halt to these actions (Barry, 1997). When Sega refused, the Almaamy, demonstrating both will and faith, invaded Bundu, captured Sega, and executed him after a brief trial. He then installed his own ruler to govern according to Islamic principles (Gomez, 1992). Despite angering the local royal family, Abdul Qadir Kane's actions helped him gain a devoted following among Muslims, who appreciated his commitment to applying Islamic law equitably.

When Ibrahima Sori (d. 1781) succeeded the revered Karamoka Alfa (d. 1751) as Almaamy, he pursued a different path. Unlike Karamoka Alfa, who sought to abolish the slave trade, Ibrahima Sori expanded military expeditions and slave raids, increasing his wealth but earning the hatred of many (Rodney, 1968). The Futa Jallon electoral council ultimately voted to replace him with Abdullah Ba Demba, the son of Karamoka Alfa (Rodney, 1968). However, Ibrahima Sori, with political savvy and ruthlessness, maintained his grip on power. Upon being summoned to the council chambers, he arrived with his army and executed those who opposed him. He then filled the resulting vacancies with his supporters, consolidating his control over the council and the region of Futa Jallon (Rodney, 1968).

ORGANIZATION AND ADMINISTRATION

Sound organization is essential to the success of any enterprise, and in the context of statecraft, such as in matters of war

PERSONALIST RULE: MAINTAINING CALIPHAL POWER

and peace, it becomes crucial. During West Africa's Classical Islamic period, Caliphs employed a variety of organizational principles to manage their expanding Islamic polities. These included establishing a central philosophy and empowering subordinates with opportunities to address grievances and translate ideas into actions, key strategies for maintaining power. This section will explore how Caliphs also employed non-managerial strategies, such as the use of language, mythology, and understanding local contexts, to strengthen their control.

Sheikh al-Hajj Umar Tall (d. 1864) created a vast empire that, at its height, spanned over 200,000 square miles. He appointed skilled leaders and devoted Muslims to positions of authority across his domain. Many individuals he advanced to these roles were of the highest caliber and could have performed excellently in the highest offices as well. For example, Almaamy Sa'ada, leader of the Islamic state of Bundu, swore allegiance to Sheikh Umar Tall and placed his family under his tutelage (Willis, 1989). Several members of his leadership circle were known for their scholarly achievements and military prowess. As an illustration, Umar Tall had one of his lieutenants, Mukhtar b. Wadi' at Allah (also known as Yarki Talfi), compose a literary masterpiece, *What Will Make al-Bakka'i Weep* (Willis, 1989). This work successfully refuted and educated one of Tall's most formidable theological opponents, helping him gain the support of scholars who were previously undecided.

As Caliphs of the Songhay Empire, both Sunni Ali and Askia Muhammad demonstrated sound organizational and management skills, enabling them to develop one of the largest and most well-organized empires in West Africa (and indeed, the world) up to that time.

A letter written by Caliph Sheikhu Ahmadu of the Massina Caliphate further exemplifies the importance African Caliphs placed on an efficient organization, grounded in merit and ability. When a well-born man complained about being passed over for a provincial leadership position, the Caliph responded as follows:

> The Council decided to monitor the security and the good administration of the Dina, so nobody unable to read, write and understand the meaning of a document written in Arabic characters can govern a territory that extends for more than five days' walk... The Council does not contest your illustrious birth, nor your military achievements. However, it would be an issue to give you an office in which neither military merit nor origin matter. From administrators we require piety and science. And, without insulting you, your piety is mild, and your science is non-existent (Nobili, 2020, p. 213).

In a stroke of political brilliance, Sultan Muhammad Bello demonstrated that all politics are local. His father, the visionary Sheikh Usman dan Fodio, advocated for a small, limited government. However, upon succeeding his father as Caliph, Sultan Muhammad Bello created a vast administrative apparatus similar in scope to the former Hausa governments. This approach ensured familiarity with the majority Hausa population while also reinforcing his authority. By adopting a Hausa-style administration, Bello cemented the political and social relationship between the Hausa and Fulani, a bond that persists to this day.

Sheikh Usman dan Fodio, the founder of the Sokoto Caliphate, had established a system during his revolution that involved distributing flags to those who pledged loyalty to the cause of Islam (Last, 1967). These flags conferred legitimacy upon generals, assuring their soldiers that Allah supported their cause. Once victorious in battle, these generals expanded the Caliphate's territory. The system of flags and the organizational structure that emerged from it played a significant role in the

PERSONALIST RULE: MAINTAINING CALIPHAL POWER

Sokoto Caliphate's prosperity and endurance (Adeleye, 1971; Last, 1967).

To expand his empire, Askia al-Hajj Muhammad of the Songhay Empire employed a strategy common in other great empires: he took many concubines from different ethnicities, thereby creating loyal constituencies. Although Islamic law limits the number of wives to four, it permits an unlimited number of concubines. These women bore his children, who often occupied important positions within their maternal homelands or stayed in the capital. This strategy allowed different ethnic groups to feel a sense of belonging within the growing empire, facilitating the integration of tribal and ethnic loyalties into the broader empire (Gomez, 2018).

Askia al-Hajj Muhammad also established a feedback system similar to the freedom of the press in modern liberal societies. Recognizing the difficulties scholars faced in speaking openly under Sunni Ali's reign, al-Hajj Muhammad reinstated scholars who had been exiled under Sunni Ali, granting them prominent roles. He encouraged learning and scholarship and permitted open critiques of his rule, enabling scholars to guide his governance in accordance with the Qur'an and the Sunnah of Prophet Muhammad.

In a display of Islamic unity, Almaamy Umar of Futa Jallon allied with Almaamy Bubakar Saada (d. 1885) of Bundu to defeat the powerful kingdom of Kaarta (Barry, 1997). Almaamy Umar organized an army of over 32,000 warriors to confront Kaarta, which adhered to a code of fighting to the last man. The Kaartan king chose to commit suicide along with his family and soldiers rather than be captured. The two leaders exhibited impressive organizational skills in assembling and maintaining such a large force, ensuring they remained fed and unified in their purpose.

Karamoka Alfa of Futa Jallon also demonstrated the importance of effective organization in maintaining his leadership. Upon becoming the newly elected leader of Futa Jallon, he instituted policies that signified a new political order. These reforms not only aligned with Islamic principles but also reflected a commitment to creating a just and orderly state. In a region plagued by kidnapping and slave raiding, Karamoka Alfa's government forbade both the enslavement of Muslims and the enslavement of non-Muslims under state protection. This stance was prescient, as thousands sought refuge in Futa Jallon, many of whom converted to Islam. Karamoka Alfa's brand of Islam became a significant barrier to the European slave trade at the time (Barry, 1997).

Futa Jallon's rise marked a significant shift toward Islamization and freedom for many. Following their victory, Futa Jallon became a federal state comprising nine provinces, each with a leader serving on a council to elect and depose the Almaamy, much like the Shura that elected Hazrat Abu Bakr Siddiq after Prophet Muhammad's death in the 7th century. A chief judge (Qadi) was appointed to ensure all policies adhered to Islamic law. Mosques and schools that provided instruction in Arabic and Islamic jurisprudence were established throughout the state. These organizational structures ensured the Almaamy's continued power and influence (Barry, 1997).

MAGNANIMITY

According to Aristotle, the "magnanimous man has what is great in every virtue" (Hardie, 1978). Rather than adopting Aristotle's broad and classical interpretation of magnanimity, this discussion focuses on specific instances of magnanimous acts that reveal the true nature of individuals. For example, the magnanimity demonstrated by some Caliphs highlights their remarkable character and astute leadership, reinforcing their greatness.

PERSONALIST RULE: MAINTAINING CALIPHAL POWER

Mai Idris Alooma (d. 1603) was one of the most magnanimous Caliphs in medieval Africa. He ruled the Kanem-Bornu Empire, located in present-day Northern Nigeria and Chad. Under his leadership, Kanem-Bornu became one of the most Islamized African states (Levtzion & Pouwels, 2000, p. 131). In a region renowned for its Islamic influence, how did this state surpass even the Sokoto Caliphate, the Songhay Empire, and other Islamic states in Futa Toro in terms of Islamization? While Mai Idris and the Kanem-Bornu Empire are not widely recognized outside Africa today, their significance remains vital.

Mai Idris was not only a great warrior and Caliph, but under his reign, Islam became deeply ingrained in the daily lives of the people of Kanem-Bornu (A.W., 1927). His leadership fostered a society where Islam was embraced across all social strata, from the humblest to the most powerful. Mai Idris was also a scholar, ascetic, warrior, jurist, Imam, and state administrator (A.W., 1927). His piety and devotion to Islam served as a model for his people. According to Levtzion and Pouwels (2000), he supported scholars and attracted students from across the Islamic world to his capital. His progressive approach to governance integrated Muslims from diverse regions and ethnic backgrounds, creating a sense of belonging among non-Kanuri and Bornu peoples.

Under Mai Idris, Islamic law was applied uniformly and justly, regardless of ethnicity, status, or social position. In stark contrast to many modern industrialized nations, where laws often favor the wealthy and powerful, Kanem-Bornu was a society where justice prevailed. Mai Idris's military strength ensured that any breaches of law were swiftly addressed. His armies, known for their resolve, never retreated until victory was achieved, even in the face of significant hardships.

The Hajj of Mansa Kankan Musa (Mansa Musa) and Askia Muhammad were also marked by magnanimity. Mansa Musa's legendary pilgrimage to Mecca raised global awareness of West Africa (Gomez, 2018). His entourage included thousands of soldiers, traders, slaves, and scholars, along with abundant gold that captured the world's attention. Mansa Musa's generosity extended to funding a house in Mecca for West African pilgrims and constructing mosques along his journey back to Mali. Though less frequently discussed, Askia Muhammad's Hajj was equally significant. According to Gomez (2018), Muhammad's contributions during his pilgrimage exceeded those of his predecessor, Mansa Musa. Both Hajj pilgrimages demonstrated the leaders' commitment to Islam and their desire to showcase the strength of their West African Islamic kingdoms on the world stage.

Muhammad Bello's reign and character also exemplified magnanimity. One notable act of courage and kinship occurred when Bello came to the aid of his uncle, Sheikh Abdullahi dan Fodio, during a battle where Abdullahi faced defeat. Despite a strained relationship due to a succession dispute, Bello put aside his differences and saved Abdullahi's emirate. This act of loyalty earned him Abdullahi's recognition as Caliph and his allegiance. Bello could have remained indifferent, but instead, he showed magnanimity, securing the loyalty of one of the most respected jurists in the Hausa lands.

Sheikh Ahmadu Kabir (d. 1897) of the Tukulor Empire inherited the mantle of leadership after his father, Sheikh al-Hajj Umar Tall, passed away. In a highly publicized ceremony, his father appointed him as his successor (Robinson, 1985). However, this did not prevent his brothers from contesting the succession, seeking to claim leadership for themselves (Hanson, 1996). Ahmadu Kabir had to wage military campaigns against his own family and former allies to secure his position. His efforts were ultimately successful, and he imprisoned his brothers. Throughout this tumultuous period, he demonstrated his superior Islamic knowledge, discipline, and piety. His personal character, which mirrored that of his father, earned him the confidence of his father to name him successor. Ahmadu Kabir's magnanimity, both in character and action, enabled him to navigate these challenges and maintain his leadership.

STRATEGIC THINKING

Another key tool in the West African Caliphs' arsenal for maintaining power was their ability to think and act strategically. Despite the limited attention in academic literature regarding the leadership strategies of West African Caliphs, their capacity for strategic thinking in the political realm has been greatly underappreciated. Whether as religious revivalists or secular rulers, these leaders articulated guiding principles for their respective polities and demonstrated the ability and resolve to implement domestic and international policies to bring these ideas to fruition. In this section, we explore how they also utilized other underappreciated managerial skills, including language mastery and an understanding of local contexts, to their advantage.

Understanding the significance of Timbuktu, Sunni Ali waited until the city's governor requested his help in overthrowing the Tuaregs. Sunni Ali successfully assisted in defeating the Tuaregs but then took control of the famed city himself (Gomez, 2018). This maneuver not only granted him control of a crucial city with strategic access to important trade routes and a reputation for scholarship, but it also solidified his legacy as the leader of West Africa's largest state at the time.

Maka Jiba (d. 1764) of Bundu, known for his fondness for alcohol (Gomez, 1992), faced a threat of war from the Almamy of Futa Jallon, Ibrahima Sori, unless he ceased drinking. Rather than risking conflict over a practice forbidden in Islam,

Maka Jiba chose to stop drinking. This decision proved to be a costless way to avoid war with a jihadist and revolutionary Islamic state.

Bokar Saada (d. 1885) of Bundu played a masterful strategic role during a critical and hostile period in West African history. He contended with French and English colonial powers, as well as the jihadist forces of Sheikh Umar Tall and other Islamic revolutionary movements in the Senegambian region. Recognizing the French threat early, he forged an alliance with them, which helped him gain the throne. However, he also negotiated with the English, who provided him with superior weaponry (Barry, 1997). When the jihad of Sheikh Umar Tall gained momentum, many of Bokar Saada's subjects rallied to Tall's call for Islamic reform. However, Bokar Saada, ever the statesman, viewed Umar Tall's jihad as a threat to Bundu's sovereignty. Instead of joining Umar Tall, he chose to remain neutral (Barry, 1997). His instincts proved correct: not only did Umar Tall lose his struggle against the French, but many of Bundu's royal contenders (particularly the Sissibe family, descendants of Malik Sy) perished in the conflict. This left Bokar Saada as the sole legitimate heir when the throne became vacant (Barry, 1997).

Almaamy Ibrahima Sori (d. 1784) overcame both a formidable army and the betrayal of a key ally. Through a mix of ferocity, strategic restraint, and maneuvering, he achieved success. Had it not been for his heroic efforts, Futa Jallon's story might have ended before it truly began (Barry, 1997, p. 99).

Muhammad Bello of Sokoto employed a strategy similar to that of early Muslims following their conquests of Syria, Persia, and North Africa in the 7th century. To defend the caliphate, he established walled towns along its frontiers. These 'ribats' served as defensive bases against foreign invasions (Last, 1967). The Sokoto Caliphate thrived under Muhammad Bello not only due to his military prowess but also his diplomatic acumen. One of his most underappreciated policies involved the Tuareg units outside Sokoto's borders. Instead of relying on military force, he negotiated treaties, which secured Sokoto's frontiers while preventing the caliphate's army from being overstretched (Last, 1967).

Maba Diakhou (d. 1867) of Jolof skillfully forged alliances with powerful regional entities, such as the Trarza Moors and Futa Toro, to unite Senegambia under a single political entity (Quinn, 1972). His strategic foresight brought him closer than anyone before him to achieving this goal.

Bokar Saada of Bundu was not known for kindness or gentleness toward his subjects. In fact, one of the principal reasons for his prolonged reign was his oppressive fiscal policies (Barry, 1997). His heavy taxation kept his subjects too preoccupied with survival to challenge his rule, and military service was mandatory. His constant wartime policies kept his state in a perpetual state of activity, preventing idleness and potential dissent. Bokar Saada understood that idle subjects might challenge his authority, so he kept them engaged in military campaigns, furthering his personal ambitions.

Almaamy Abdul Qadir Kane used unoccupied land as a means to gain support from powerful factions in Futa Toro (Barry, 1997). This strategy helped him rally resources for new campaigns to expand his polity. During a time of widespread slave raiding, he forbade the sale or capture of Muslims within his realm, offering Islam as a shield against the slave trade. This policy played a significant role in the spread of Islam in West Africa, as individuals and entire communities converted to avoid enslavement.

King Lat Sukaabe (d. 1886) of Kajoor integrated religious and political interests within his kingdom. Rather than isolating religious clerics from courtly affairs, he appointed them to official positions, including strategic territorial commanderies. They were also expected to march with the king's army during wartime (Colvin, 1975). For the first time in Kajoor's history, Islamic clerics were allowed to marry into royal families, strengthening ties with prominent Islamic leaders. These policies facilitated peace between the monarchy and the Islamic forces, fostering harmony and stability throughout his reign (Colvin, 1975).

Similar to Lat Sukaabe, Sultan Muhammadu Rumfa (d. 1499) of the Kano Kingdom integrated the rising religion of Islam into the social fabric of his realm. To advance this integration, he chopped down the kingdom's symbolic ritual tree and built a mosque in its place. He welcomed prominent Islamic jurists, including Abd al-Karim al-Maghili (d. 1505), and sought their guidance on Islamic governance. Al-Maghili's advice was later formalized in a renowned treatise concerning the obligation of prices. Rumfa remained acutely aware of key Islamic officials traveling through his kingdom. When he learned that the scholar, Abd al-Rahman from Mali, had entered Kano on his way to the pilgrimage in Mecca, Rumfa invited him to remain and make Kano his permanent residence (Sanneh, 2016). Abd al-Rahman and his entourage agreed (Sanneh, 2016). Through these actions, Rumfa strategically transformed his kingdom into a center of Islamic learning, erudition, and practice. This development was significant because it contributed to regional stability during a period of considerable social and political change.

CONCLUSION

This chapter explored the key factors that enabled African Caliphs to maintain their power through the lens of personalist rule. Unlike contemporary electoral systems, where norms, rules, and institutions play a crucial role in sustaining leadership, African Caliphs were often dependent solely on themselves and, frequently, their religion. As human leaders, African Caliphs were not immune to fallibility. However, they had to leverage every available resource to sustain their rule. This examination reveals the diverse strategies employed by Muslim leaders in political leadership. Stereotypes about Black leaders in Africa and the African Diaspora persist, yet this chapter highlights the varied approaches African Caliphs used to maintain power. Some Caliphs operated within the constraints of ethnic institutions and Islamic traditions, while others acted with greater autonomy. While the analysis spans several centuries (11th–19th), the core factors that enabled African Caliphs to maintain power appear consistent. This consistency is also reflected in existing scholarship on African Muslim leaders of the period, though it may not explicitly use the same terminology. Key factors, such as outward displays of faith and piety (including strict adherence to prayer), magnanimity (including charisma and confidence), sound organization, and strategic thinking, are recurrent elements in the political strategies of African Caliphs. This chapter makes a significant contribution to the study of African political leadership by offering valuable insights into the strategic and multifaceted methods through which West African Caliphs maintained power. These insights are particularly beneficial for scholars and students of African political history, Islamic governance, and the broader dynamics of power and leadership.

REFERENCES

Adeleye, R. A. (1971). *Power and diplomacy in northern Nigeria, 1804–1906: The Sokoto caliphate and its enemies.* London: Longman.

A. W. (1927). History of the first twelve years of the reign of Mai Idris, Alooma of Bornu (1571–1583). *African Affairs, 27*(CV), 90.

Barry, B. (1997). *Senegambia and the Atlantic slave trade*. Cambridge: Cambridge University Press.

Bueno de Mesquita, B., Morrow, J. D., Siverson, R. M., & Smith, A. (1999). An institutional explanation of the democratic peace. *American Political Science Review, 93*(4), 791–807.

Charles, E. A. (1977). *Precolonial Senegal: The Jolof Kingdom, 1800–1890* (African Research Studies, no. 12). Boston: African Studies Center, Boston University.

Colvin, L. G. (1975). International relations in precolonial Senegambia. *Présence Africaine, 93*, 215–230.

Fenno, R. F. (1978). *Home style: House members in their districts*. Little & Brown.

Fisher, H. J. (1971). Prayer and military activity in the history of Muslim Africa south of the Sahara. *The Journal of African History, 12*(3), 391–406.

Gomez, M. (2018). *African dominion: A new history of empire in early and medieval West Africa*. Princeton University Press.

Gomez, M. (1992). *Pragmatism in the age of jihad: The precolonial state of Bundu*. Cambridge: Cambridge University Press.

Hanson, J. (1996). *Migration, jihad, and Muslim authority in West Africa: The Futanke colonies in Kaarta*. Bloomington and Indianapolis: Indiana University Press.

Hardie, W. F. R. (1978). "Magnanimity" in Aristotle's *Ethics. Phronesis, 23*(1), 63–79.

Last, M. (1967). *The Sokoto caliphate*. London: Longmans, Green, and Co. Ltd.

Levtzion, N., & Pouwels, R. L. (Eds.). (2000). *The history of Islam in Africa*. Cape Town: Oxford University Press.

Mayhew, D. (1974). *Congress: The electoral connection*. Yale University Press.

Nobili, M. (2020). Sultan, caliph, and the renewer of the faith: Aḥmad Lobbo, the *Tārīkh al-Fattāsh* and the making of an Islamic state in West Africa. *Cambridge University Press*.

Person, Y. (1979). *Samori and Islam*. In J. Willis. (Ed.), *Studies in West African Islamic History: The Cultivators of Islam* (pp. 259–277). Routledge.

Robinson, D. (1973). Abdul Qadir and Shaykh Umar: A continuing tradition of Islamic leadership in Futa Toro. *The International Journal of African Historical Studies, 6*(2), 286–303.

Robinson, D. (1985). *The holy war of Umar Tal: The Western Sudan in the mid-nineteenth century.* Oxford: Clarendon Press.

Rodney, W. (1968). Jihad and social revolution in Futa Djalon in the eighteenth century. *Journal of the Historical Society of Nigeria, 4*(2), 269–284.

Sanneh, Lamin. (2016). *Beyond jihad: The pacifist tradition in West African Islam.* New York: Oxford University Press.

Sulaiman, I. (2009). *The African Caliphate: The life works & teachings of Shaykh Usman Dan Fodio (1754–1817).* London: The Diwan Press Ltd.

Theiler, T. (2017). Political symbolism. In F. M. Moghaddam (Ed.), *The SAGE Encyclopedia of Political Behavior.* Thousand Oaks: SAGE Publications.

Ware, R. T. (2013). *The walking Qur'an: Islamic education, embodied knowledge, and history in West Africa.* University of North Carolina Press.

Willis, J. (1989). *In the path of Allah: The passion of Al-Hajj Umar: An essay into the nature of charisma in Islam.* 2 Park Square, Milton Park, Abingdon, Oxon: Frank Cass & Co. Ltd.

CHAPTER 6

LOSING CALIPHAL POWER

Sheikh Umar of the Kanem-Borno Empire

Ueberreichung der Geschenke König Wilhelm's an Scheïch 'Omar von Bornû. (S. 594.)

CHAPTER 6

PERSONALIST RULE: LOSING CALIPHAL POWER

This chapter provides an insightful and rich examination of the factors leading to the loss of political power among African Caliphs, with a particular focus on internal political dynamics and external colonial pressures. It paints a vivid picture of the complex and multifaceted nature of political power in West Africa's Classical Islamic period. Understanding how political power is lost is as valuable as knowing how it is acquired and maintained. Leaders who comprehend the dynamics of losing power are better positioned to prevent such outcomes. Similarly, the general populace can use this knowledge to challenge the unjust actions of rulers, particularly when they understand how to remove political power from them. As it now stands, theories explaining the loss of political power during West Africa's Classical Islamic period (and precolonial period in general) remain relatively sparse within the literature. Although scholars have effectively documented individual episodes of West African leaders losing power within specific political systems, developing broader theories to explain this phenomenon would provide a more complete understanding of Black political leadership.

While theories on losing political power are less numerous than those on acquiring it, several frameworks exist to conceptualize why political elites lose power. Mayhew (1974) offers one of the most enduring theories, arguing that political leaders prioritize reelection or maintaining power above all else. Any decision that threatens their chances of remaining in office renders them vulnerable to removal. Fenno (1978) provides additional insight, focusing on members of Congress. He suggests that political leaders categorize their constituencies into four concentric circles: the geographic constituency, the reelection constituency, the primary constituency, and the personal constituency. Leaders must develop strategies to satisfy these groups, and failure to do so risks losing political support. Fenno's theory highlights the importance of maintaining trust and cooperation through a leader's personal "homestyle." Mayhew's (1974) theory has endured across disciplines, influencing theories in International Relations. For instance, selectorate theory, as presented by Bueno de Mesquita et al. (2003), asserts that leaders who fail to satisfy their winning coalition are more likely to lose power. Weeks (2008) extends this idea by demonstrating that audience costs apply not only to democratic leaders but also to authoritarian rulers, who ignore these costs at their peril.

This study examines the loss of political power by Caliphs, focusing on the internal factors contributing to their downfall. Broadly, Caliphal loss of power can be categorized into four main causes: revolution, war, deposition, and colonialism. While colonialism had a limited role in the acquisition and maintenance of power, it played a significant role in the decline of African Caliphs. However, this study prioritizes the political dynamics of African Caliphs over European colonial influence. Deposition, often akin to a coup d'état, includes both forced removal from office and the voluntary relinquishment of power due to age or incapacity.

Table 4 shows that 43% of the Caliphs in West Africa's Classical Islamic period lost power due to deposition.

PERSONALIST RULE: LOSING CALIPHAL POWER

Deposition could involve a coup, removal by high-ranking officials, or being deemed unfit to rule. Deposition does not always result in death, as some deposed Caliphs were allowed to return to power. Additionally, 21% of the observed Caliphs lost power due to colonialism, which typically involved being defeated in battle, deposed, or killed by a European colonial power. Most of these Caliphs were deposed by the French, who controlled the largest colonial territory in West Africa by the late 19th century. In their pursuit of territory and resources, the French eliminated several Caliphs perceived as threats. Furthermore, 20% of the Caliphs lost power due to military defeat, either dying on the battlefield or being stripped of their title after a military loss. Many Caliphs lost power amid the Islamic revolutions of the 18th century (Lovejoy, 2016). While military defeat often led to deposition, these two causes are considered separately for analytical clarity. Indeed, 14% of the Caliphs in Table 4 lost power due to revolution. This may seem surprising given the prominence of revolutions in the literature on Islamic politics in West Africa. However, revolutions in this region were typically isolated events, whereas deposition by family members was a more continuous process.

Table 4 African Caliphs and the Methods by which their Political Authority was Lost

Military Defeat/ Killed in Action	Revolution	Colonialism	Deposed
Maba Diakhou Ba (Rip & Jolof)	Ahmadu Seku III (Caliphate of Massina)	Umar Tall (Tukulor Empire)	Shehu Umar (Kanem & Borno Empire)
Abdul Qadir Khan (Futa Toro)	Muhammadu Hodi (Kebbi)	Ahmad Kabir (Tukulor Empire)	Shehu Abdurrahman (Kanem & Borno Empire)

THE AFRICAN CALIPHS

Shehu Sanda Limannambe (Kanem & Borno Empire)	Muhamman Makau (Zaria Kingdom)	Boko Biro (Imamate of Futa Jallon)	Mansa Khalifa Keita (Empire of Mali)
Shehu Kiari (Kanem & Borno Empire)	Gwari Abdu (Daura)	Ahmadou of Timbo	Sakura (Empire of Mali)
Bubu Malik (Imamate of Bundu)	Magajin Halidu (Katsina Kingdom)	Samori Ture (Wassalou Empire)	Mansa Maghan I (Empire of Mali)
Maka Jiba (Imamate of Bundu)	Muhammad Alwal II (Kano Kingdom)	Almamy Alfa Yaya (Labe)	Mansa Qassa (Empire of Mali)
Umar Penda (Imamate of Bundu)	Yunfa (Gobir Kingdom)	Saleh (Bedde)	Mansa Fadima Musa (Empire of Mali)
Mansa Mahmud Keita IV (Empire of Mali)	Majiya (Nupe Kingdom)	Lat Dior (Jolof Kingdom)	Mansa Sandaki (Empire of Mali)
Musa Ule Sise (Imamate of Medina)		Mamadou Lamine	Askia al-Hajj Muhammad (Songhay Empire)
Umar Sane (Imamate of Bundu)		Musa Molo (Imamate of Fulado)	
Tumane Mudi (Imamate of Bundu)		Fode Kaba (Imamate of Medina)	Sunni Baru (Songhay Empire)
		Albury N'Diaye (Jolof Kingdom)	Shehu Ashimi (Kenem & Borno Empire)

PERSONALIST RULE: LOSING CALIPHAL POWER

		Muhammadu Attahiru I (Sokoto Caliphate)	Samba Tumane (Imamate of Bundu)
			Sega Gai (Imamate of Bundu)
			Saada Amdai (Imamate Bundu)
			Dakauta (Kano Kingdom)
			Atuma (Kano Kingdom)
			Yakufu (Kano Kingdom)
			Dauda Abasama (Kano Kingdom)
			Abubakar Kado (Kano Kingdom)
			Muhamman Shashere (Kano Kingdom)
			Alhaji (Kano Kingdom)
			Muhamman Kukuna (Kano)
			Soyaki (Kano)
			Muhamma Alwali (Kano)

To understand the factors contributing to the loss of power by African Caliphs, it is necessary to scrutinize the actions and behaviors of the leaders involved. I categorize these actions into three main areas: (1) administrative issues, (2) family issues, and (3) strategic blunders. Administrative issues relate to bureaucratic and management decisions, as well as executive actions. Family issues concern succession disputes and internal conflicts within ruling families. Strategic blunders refer to avoidable, costly mistakes that result from a lack of prudence.

ADMINISTRATIVE ISSUES

The first issue to address is administrative challenges. As Buena de Mesquita et al. (2003) note, one of the most common administrative missteps leading to a loss of political support and power is the failure to properly distribute private goods to one's winning coalition. For example, Shehu Umar (d. 1881), the Shehu and leader of the Bornu Empire, was deposed by his brother, Abdurrahman (d. 1854), due to the former's decision to withhold spoils from a strenuous military campaign (Brenner, 1973). However, Abdurrahman would soon be overthrown by his own people, who cited his cruelty, indulgence in pleasure-seeking, and ruthless exploitation of the masses as key reasons for his downfall. Thus, despite deposing his brother for failing to share the spoils of war, Abdurrahman committed the same error against those who had helped him ascend to power, leading to his own deposition (Brenner, 1973).

Similarly, Askia Benkan (d. 1559), Caliph of the Songhay Empire, faced consequences for failing to reward Muhammadu Kanta (d. 1561), one of his most capable military captains. As a result, Kanta established his own polity in Kebbi (now part of northern Nigeria). Despite repeated attempts by Askia

PERSONALIST RULE: LOSING CALIPHAL POWER

Benkan to regain control of Kebbi, his efforts failed. This failure became intolerable for the proud members of West Africa's most formidable military at the time. Askia Benkan was soon deposed following his inability to reclaim the important kingdom of Kebbi. Had he distributed the spoils of war more judiciously, he could have retained control of this strategic territory, his most able captain, and his throne (Gomez, 2018).

Leadership requires acting from positions of strength, particularly when betraying a senior member of one's administration. To attempt such a betrayal from a position of weakness only increases the likelihood of failure, strengthening the hand of the betrayed individual. For example, after suffering a significant military defeat, Songhay leader Askia Muhammad Bonkana Kirya sought to betray one of his senior governors (Hunwick, 1999). The Askia had been severely wounded and, to make a successful retreat, had to be carried through a swamp by one of his officials. He sent the governor on a mission but secretly followed him with members of his inner circle. However, the governor discovered the spies, shackled them in iron chains, and ultimately deposed the Askia (Hunwick, 1999).

Umar Penda of Bundu also committed a serious administrative error at a critical moment. In his conflict with the Islamic reformer Mamadu Lamine, Umar Penda attempted to ambush Lamine's forces along their usual route. However, he foolishly sent the bulk of his forces to that location, leaving himself and his family vulnerable. Lamine, having anticipated this move, sent his forces by an alternate route, and Umar Penda, lacking sufficient defenders, was killed along with his remaining followers. His wife, children, and slaves were taken into captivity (Gomez, 1993). While taking risks is part of leadership, leaving oneself and one's family unprotected during times of conflict can be disastrous.

Similarly, the Damel (king) of Kajoor, Detie Maram, made a grave administrative mistake when he deposed a prominent Queen Mother. In retaliation, she formed a marriage alliance with Ndyai Sal, a powerful Islamic judge and counselor to the king. Together, they orchestrated the king's assassination and installed their own candidate on the throne (Colvin, 1974). This incident underscores the importance of carefully managing administrative appointments, as the removal of influential individuals can have dire consequences.

When Ahmad al-Kabir (d.1897), the firstborn son of Sheikh al-Hajj Umar Tall, succeeded his father as leader of the vast Tukulor Empire, he inherited significant challenges. Al-Kabir was the son of al-Hajj Umar Tall and a Sokoto princess, a union that tied the Tukulor Empire to the Sokoto Caliphate. After al-Hajj Umar Tall was martyred in battle against the French, a generation of leaders, teachers, and warriors perished with him (Robinson, 1985). From the outset, Sheikh Ahmad al-Kabir had little room for error. Despite his father's public ceremony naming him successor, his brothers, rooted in the Senegambia region, rebelled against him, believing their heritage should carry more weight. However, it was not his brothers who ultimately led to his downfall. After defeating them and securing the loyalty of his other siblings, Sheikh Ahmad's fate was sealed by the French desire to control the region. The garrisoned towns that formed the backbone of the Tukulor Empire proved inadequate in responding to French incursions. While garrisoned towns may have worked for smaller, less populous kingdoms, the expansive Tukulor Empire, with its large and hostile populations, required a more substantial military presence. Despite his long tenure of over 30 years maintaining law and order, Sheikh Ahmad could not withstand the French strategy of systematically capturing the garrisoned towns. Ultimately, he retreated to

Sokoto, near his mother's village, with about 1,000 followers, where he died after a brief illness (Robinson, 1985). Of all the Caliphs capable of resisting European encroachment, Al-Kabir was perhaps the best positioned. With his vast empire, extensive weaponry, and experienced veterans, a more comprehensive strategy could have prevented his territory from being gradually lost.

Sega Gai (d. 1797) of Bundu made a critical error in his administration by failing to adopt Islamic policies, which were particularly significant in a region where the powerful Islamic reformer Almaamy Abdul Qadir Khan ruled next door. For instance, Sega Gai shocked his Muslim subjects by entering a mosque after engaging in relations with his wife without performing the required ritual purification (Gomez, 1993). Additionally, he continued practices such as the non-Islamic Bambara dance, which antagonized Abdul Qadir Khan (Gomez, 1993). In his efforts to suppress a growing uprising, Sega Gai attacked several Muslim villages and sold many of the inhabitants into slavery, a clear violation of Islamic law. This infuriated Abdul Qadir Khan, who met Sega Gai in battle and decisively defeated him. Abdul Qadir Khan then convened a council to determine the appropriate punishment for Sega Gai's transgressions, and the council voted to have him executed. In front of his own people, Abdul Qadir Khan immediately carried out the death sentence (Gomez, 1993).

FAMILY ISSUES

Family dynamics were a significant and consistent cause of political instability among African Caliphs, often contributing to their loss of the throne. In particular, competition among siblings for leadership was a key factor in the political downfall of Caliphs during West Africa's Classical Islamic

Age. However, internal family conflict, beyond sibling rivalry, also played a crucial role. Disputes among uncles, fathers, and other relatives were often pivotal in undermining Caliphs' power.

A notable example is the case of Askia Muhammad (d. 1538), whose appointment of a relatively unknown individual as governor of a prestigious province enraged his son, Musa, who had expected the position. Upon investigation, Musa discovered that his father's most trusted and ambitious advisors had influenced the decision. Moreover, Musa learned that Askia Muhammad had been blind for some time. Seizing on this knowledge, Musa and his supporters deposed his father and sent him into a "peaceful" retirement. Although Musa spared his father's life, his actions sparked a civil war, during which he killed 30-40 of his brothers and cousins to solidify his claim to the throne. Musa even killed his uncle, who had attempted to reconcile father and son. Despite his brutal path to power, the consequences were severe. Musa was assassinated by a coalition of his remaining brothers, led by Mohammad Benkan and Alu Way, after a two-day revolt. Alu Way delivered the fatal blow, ending Musa's two-year, tumultuous reign. After his death, Mohammad Benkan succeeded him as Askia. Thus, Musa's fratricidal actions paved the way for his own downfall.

Samba Tumane's (r. 1764) brief rule as the leader of the Imamate of Bundu was similarly shaped by family conflicts. His deposition resulted not from his own actions but from those of his father. When the former leader of Bundu sought military assistance from his brother (Samba Tumane's father), the latter refused, leading to the former's defeat and death. Following this, Samba Tumane was elected leader but soon faced opposition from powerful family members who deposed him and exiled him to a neighboring state (Gomez, 1987).

PERSONALIST RULE: LOSING CALIPHAL POWER

STRATEGIC AND COSTLY MISTAKES

Strategic mistakes arise from poor planning, organization, and foresight, while costly mistakes are the result of errors in judgment. These errors often stem from misassessing significant situations or even simple lapses in judgment. Although political leaders are typically regarded as rational actors, they, like all humans, are susceptible to emotions, impulsiveness, and psychological issues that can adversely impact their decision-making. Political actors must rely on the information available to make decisions. Unfortunately, no one has access to all relevant information, and political leaders must often make do with limited data. While this can sometimes be sufficient, at other times, it can be highly detrimental.

Almaamy Maka Jiba (d. 1764) of Bundu made a costly strategic mistake when he waged a siege against a hostile nation and was forced to retreat. During his retreat, the Almaamy's turban became entangled in a tree branch. Faced with the choice of securing a successful retreat or retrieving his beautiful turban, he prioritized the latter, which ultimately cost him his life (Gomez, 1993).

Almaamy Abdul Qadir Khan (d. 1806) of Futa Toro lost power by overestimating the loyalty of the peoples he had conquered and forced into his armies. For example, he demanded the leader of Waalo pledge allegiance to his suzerainty and Islamic leadership over the Muslim faithful. Although the Waalo leader outwardly complied, he secretly plotted to break away. When the Almaamy conscripted personnel from all his dominions to fight a major war, the Waalo leader sent soldiers who only answered to him. Upon reaching the battlefield, these soldiers defected to the enemy, leading to a devastating defeat for the Almaamy. His soldiers were executed or sold into slavery, and the Almaamy himself was taken prisoner. Though he was later released, his reputation and integrity were severely diminished. The elderly Almaamy continued to lead Futa Toro but, despite his age, would again launch an expedition. On this occasion, not only did his forces lose, but he was also executed by the brother of a Muslim leader he had killed in cold blood.

Ma Fali, King of Kajoor, was caught by Islamic clerics drinking alcohol, an act that led to his execution and replacement due to his failure to understand the religious tide within his kingdom (Curtin, 1971).

Amid the crisis, the blind and aging Mai Ahmad (d. 1808) of the Kanem-Bornu Empire lost vast territory to the invading revolutionary forces of the Sokoto Caliphate. Believing he could no longer rule effectively, Mai Ahmad voluntarily abdicated in favor of his son, Dunama. The people of the empire, however, viewed this as improper because a Mai was expected to rule until death. This decision would sow the seeds of instability, as it legitimized the transfer of power during times of crisis. Mai Dunama, with the support of a popular cleric, Muhammad al-Kanemi, won several decisive battles and repelled the invaders. However, Dunama's constant relocation and his inability to project confidence undermined his rule. He was eventually deposed by his uncle, Mai Ngilruma, who argued that Dunama's enthronement was invalid because the previous Mai was still alive (Brenner, 1973).

Once back on the throne, Mai Dunama (d. 1817) made the mistake of relying on Muhammad al-Kanemi, a highly ambitious figure. To protect his kingdom from the jihad of Usman dan Fodio, Mai Dunama enlisted al-Kanemi's aid. Al-Kanemi not only resisted the jihadists on religious grounds but also repelled the invaders through military skill and quelled internal revolutionaries. However, Mai Dunama's dependence on al-Kanemi ultimately led to his downfall. As al-Kanemi gained control of the military, the troops and the people began to view him as the true leader. Eventually, al-Kanemi seized control of the kingdom.

Albuuri Njay (d. 1901) of the Jolof Kingdom was one of the most formidable opponents of French encroachment in the Senegambian region. He skillfully navigated between ally and adversary roles with the French, thus prolonging his kingdom's independence. However, his downfall came from his support of Lat Dior of Kayor, a longtime French adversary. According to Charles (1977), after a decade of impressive military and diplomatic leadership, Albuuri Njay's rivals had failed to defeat him. As he extended his influence to other Muslim rulers opposing French expansion, the French viewed him as too great a threat to remain in Jolof.

Mamadou Lamine (d. 1887), ruler of Bundu, mistakenly believed that a raid on a village near French interests would not be perceived as an act of aggression (Gomez, 1993, p. 163). He was wrong. The French rejected his conciliatory offers and continued their campaign against him until he was no longer deemed a threat. His unnecessary attack proved costly. Sunni Ali of the Songhay Empire met his demise after miscalculating his crossing of the Niger River following a successful military campaign. Having never lost a battle, the people considered him to be invincible. Unfortunately, failing to properly prepare against the Niger River brought this streak to an end. Mansa Mahmud Keita IV, the last great emperor of the Mali Empire, failed to restore Mali's former glory after the fall of the Songhay Empire to Moroccan and Southern European armies. Instead of learning from Songhay's mistakes, Mali repeated them. Mansa Mahmud Keita IV launched a full-scale attack without adequate intelligence on his foes' capabilities and resources, nor did he acquire the new firearms his opponents were using. As a result, Mali lost its status as West Africa's greatest power, and Mansa Mahmud Keita IV was forced to flee deeper into his territory.

Sunni Ali (d. 1492) of the Songhay Empire met his demise after miscalculating his crossing of the Niger River following a successful military campaign. Having never lost a battle, his subjects regarded him as invincible. This reputation ended when his failure to prepare adequately for the river crossing proved fatal.

Mansa Mahmud Keita IV (r. 1550–1599), the last great emperor of the Mali Empire, similarly failed to restore Mali's former power after the defeat of the Songhay Empire by Moroccan and Southern European forces. Rather than learning from Songhay's collapse, Mali repeated its strategic errors. Mansa Mahmud Keita IV launched a full-scale attack without sufficient intelligence regarding his opponents' capabilities and resources and without acquiring the firearms they employed. Consequently, Mali lost its status as West Africa's preeminent power, and Mansa Mahmud Keita IV was forced to retreat deeper into his territory.

Mori Ule Sise (r. 1830s–1870s), who established an Islamic state in the southern region of Futa Toro, made a crucial miscalculation. Despite his success in spreading Islam and consolidating power, he forcefully demanded conversion from all subjects. Although his regime was initially successful, he underestimated the resistance to abandoning traditional religions and identities. The kingdom ultimately fell to forces that adopted a more conciliatory approach to the inhabitants (Person, 1979).

ONSET OF COLONIALISM

Several African Caliphates came to an end with the onset of colonialism. The French, Portuguese, and English were among the primary European powers that viewed Islam as an obstacle to their regional ambitions. For example, French forces killed prominent figures such as al-Hajj Umar Tall, Lat Dior, Albury N'diaye, Maba Diakhou, Bokar Biro, Almaamy Alfa Yaya of Labe, Ahmadou of Timbo, and Samori Ture (Barry, 1998). These assassinations had a profound negative impact on the quality of political leadership in the region. Similarly, the English executed key African Caliphs, including Caliph Muhammadu Attahiru of the Sokoto Caliphate (Last, 1967). After his death, the British installed their own "emir" until Nigeria's independence. Where once powerful kingdoms and empires reigned, European powers established colonies, mirroring the expansionist practices of the Roman Empire.

Although this study does not focus extensively on the relationship between African Caliphs and colonialism, a few observations are warranted. According to Barry (1998), the Muslim warrior Caliph represented perhaps the only legitimate challenge to colonial domination across the region. As many prominent Caliphs fell to European powers, traditional African rulers were left with limited options in their dealings with colonial authorities. The general trajectory, and subsequently later rule, tended toward collaboration and ultimately subjugation. In a region characterized by numerous long-standing traditions and diverse nationalities, traditionalist leaders often lacked a sufficiently broad message to mobilize the masses and create a unified front. Focusing on the Senegambian region, Barry (1998) notes that the "narrowness of vision, mirroring with peculiar sharpness the political fragmentation of Senegambia after the failure of the unifying efforts of nineteenth-century Muslim leaders, was the main reason why last-ditch resistance efforts against colonial occupation failed" (p. 313).

CONCLUSION

This chapter presents one of the first general surveys of the loss of political power by African Caliphs during West Africa's Classical Islamic period. Scholars often attribute this loss solely to colonialism, tribalism, and the Transatlantic Slave Trade. However, given the sheer number of Muslim states, the extended time frame, and the variety of Muslim rulers, these explanations fail to offer a comprehensive understanding of the factors that led to the downfall of Muslim leaders. Instead, multiple and diverse causes emerge across time and space.

This chapter demonstrates that, in many cases, the reasons behind an African Caliph's loss of power stem from local concerns. Most African Caliphs lost power after being deposed, but the causes of deposition varied. They were sometimes deemed too weak or corrupt, too "un-Islamic," or too old or mentally incapable. Whatever the case, the issues were often local, and thus the solutions were also local. Additionally, many Caliphs lost power due to Islamic revolutions, even when they were from revolutionary or founding families. For instance, Ahmadu Seku III of the Massina Empire, grandson of the state's founder, Sheikhu Ahmadu Lobbo, lost his kingdom after a protracted intellectual and military struggle with Sheikh al-Hajj Umar Tall's forces, culminating in the rise of the reformist Tukulor Empire (Willis, 1989). Similarly, many Muslim leaders in Hausaland lost power during the revolution led by Sheikh Usman dan Fodio (Sulaiman, 2009). One of Fodio's criticisms was that these leaders mixed traditional practices with the core tenets of Islam.

Costly mistakes, such as poor planning and errors in judgment, frequently led to the loss of power for many leaders. For example, Maka Jiba's attempt to recover his turban and

PERSONALIST RULE: LOSING CALIPHAL POWER

Almaamy Abdul Qadir Khan's overestimation of loyalty both resulted in significant political setbacks. Family dynamics, especially sibling rivalry and conflicts among relatives, were major contributors to political instability, as seen in the cases of Askia Muhammad and Samba Tumane. Administrative failures, particularly improper reward distribution, caused internal dissatisfaction and rebellion, leading to the downfall of leaders like Shehu Umar and Askia Benkan. Additionally, colonialism significantly contributed to the decline of African Caliphs, with European powers, such as the French and English, eliminating key leaders to assert control over the region.

As discussed earlier, understanding the factors that contribute to the loss of political power is as important as understanding those that help acquire and maintain it. Among the African Caliphs studied here, effective administration, strong and trustworthy family ties, and avoiding strategic errors were key to retaining power. Although revolutions often draw attention, African Caliphs were more frequently deposed from within their own circles. This highlights a critical lesson for political leaders globally: internal dissent is often the greatest threat. However, during times of revolution, leaders who adopt a pragmatic approach, either by aligning with or accommodating the revolutionaries, are more likely to secure favorable outcomes and maintain power. If joining the "winning team" is not an option, finding ways to accommodate them until the situation stabilizes may be the next best strategy. This approach was exemplified by the Caliph of Zaria, Sarki Jattau. When Sheikh Usman dan Fodio of the Sokoto Caliphate sent Sarki Jattau and the rulers of other Hausa states, particularly Katsina and Kano, a letter requesting support for his jihad and state reforms, only Jattau complied. As a result, Zaria avoided attack, whereas the leaders of Katsina and Kano were overthrown (Adeleye, 1971).

REFERENCES

Brenner, L. (1973). *The Shehus of Kukawa: A history of the Al-Kanemi dynasty of Bornu.* Clarendon Press.

Bueno de Mesquita, B., Smith, A., Siverson, R., & Morrow, J. (2003). *The logic of political survival.* The MIT Press.

Curtin, P. D. (1971). Jihad in West Africa: Early phases and inter-relations in Mauritania and Senegal. *The Journal of African History, 12*(1), 11–24.

Fenno, R. F. (1978). *Home style: House members in their districts.* Little, Brown.

Gomez, M. A. (2018). *African dominion: A new history of empire in early and medieval West Africa.* Princeton University Press.

Gomez, M. (1987). Bundu in the eighteenth century. *The International Journal of African Historical Studies, 20*(1), 61–73.

Gomez, M. (1993). *Pragmatism in the age of jihad: The precolonial state of Bundu.* Cambridge University Press.

Hunwick, J. (Ed.), & trans. (1999). *Timbuktu and the Songhay Empire: Al Sadi's Tarikh al-Sudan down to 1613 and other contemporary documents.* Brill.

Last, M. (1967). *The Sokoto Caliphate.* Longmans, Greens, and Co. Ltd.

Lovejoy, P. E. (2016). *Jihād in West Africa during the Age of Revolutions* (1st ed.). Ohio University Press.

Mayhew, D. (1974). *Congress: The electoral connection.* Yale University Press.

Person, Y. (1979). Samori and Islam. In J. R. Willis (Ed.), *Studies in West African Islamic history: The cultivators of Islam.* Routledge.

Robinson, D. (1985). *The holy war of Umar Tal: The Western Sudan in the mid-nineteenth century.* Clarendon Press.

Sulaiman, I. (2009). *The African Caliphate: The life works & teachings of Shaykh Usman Dan Fodio (1754–1817).* The Diwan Press Ltd.

Weeks, J. L. (2008). Autocratic audience costs: Regime type and signaling resolve. *International Organization, 62*(1), 35–64.

CHAPTER 7

CONCLUSION

Shehu Muhammad al-Amin al-Kanemi of the Kanem-Borno Empire

By engraver Edward Francis Finden in Dixon Denham's memoir of his travel to Bornu, *Narrative of travels and discoveries in Northern and Central Africa, in the years 1822, 1823, and 1824. Vol I* Fontpiece, (1826)

CHAPTER 7

CONCLUSION

African Caliphs, as political leaders, relied primarily on their own abilities to acquire and maintain power. When they lost power, blame was often directed at their personal failings. Like political systems elsewhere, African Caliphs operated within established political institutions and traditions, including Islam, which at times constrained their behavior. However, as in other political systems, they found ways to exploit loopholes, breach weak points, and manipulate ambiguities to further their political ambitions. Consequently, political traditions were either respected or set aside as needed. At every stage of their *game of thrones*, African Caliphs had to navigate circumstances to their advantage.

This study has focused on power and politics among African Caliphs. It demonstrates that success in acquiring, maintaining, and preventing the loss of power requires personal skill and individual-level expertise. The type of power under consideration here refers to the position of the official head of an autonomous and self-governing political unit, such as a kingdom, empire, or imamate. While political subordinates are important, this study does not focus on them. For example, although each Emirate within the Sokoto Caliphate ruled independently, all were subordinate to the Caliph of Sokoto.

To the author's knowledge, this is the only comprehensive study examining political authority among West African Muslim leaders. Given that Africa is the only continent with a Muslim-majority population, such a study is long overdue. Beyond its political insights, this work also offers a deeper appreciation and understanding of West African political life. Each chapter includes mini-sketches of African Caliphs, offering glimpses into political leadership within the Sokoto Caliphate, the revolutionary fervor of the Fulanis in Senegambia, the military dictatorship of Samori Toure, and the spiritual mission of Sheikh al-Hajj Umar Tall. While this study focuses on political leaders at the helm of their respective states, future research should consider the experiences of everyday people, women, and other members of these societies. Several excellent works address these aspects of West Africa's Classical Islamic period, and I hope to incorporate these perspectives in future studies.

A major strength of this study is its dynamic findings. By examining African Caliphs over several centuries, we avoid the limitations of a time-bound analysis. However, some may argue that the findings are outdated in the context of the post-colonial world. While this may be true to some extent, the political implications drawn from the lived experiences of African Caliphs regarding power remain enduring. The study engages with some of the oldest and most fundamental questions in politics and leadership: Who has the right to organize and rule society? What is the nature of God, and what is God's relationship to humankind? How are authoritative values established, and what obligations do people have to adhere to them? What qualities make a good statesman? Is being a good Muslim (or adherent of any faith) the sole qualification for leadership, or are other qualities also important? These questions continue to shape political life and governance today. All polities must confront them in some form.

CONCLUSION

In addressing these questions, African Caliphs provide a blueprint for approaching similar issues in contemporary political life. Their strategies for acquiring, maintaining, and losing power offer valuable lessons for modern leadership. As politics and political leadership are enduring aspects of the human experience, the search for better ways to attain power remains a timeless endeavor. By focusing on African Caliphs, this study contributes an alternative repository of solutions to contemporary challenges surrounding the quest for political power.

This study also draws on a rich body of scholarly work to create an original dataset documenting political information about African Caliphs from the 11th to the 19th centuries. Given the damaging legacy of colonialism and its efforts to dismantle the intellectual heritage of precolonial West Africa, much of this knowledge remains inaccessible. As Asante and Abarry (1996) observe, "One cannot estimate the damage done to the intellectual heritage of the continent" (p. 1). The continued exploration of these untapped resources holds great promise for future research.

REFERENCE

Asante, M. K., & Abarry, A. S. (1996). *African intellectual heritage: A book of sources.* Temple University Press.

CHAPTER 7

APPENDIX A

CHAPTER 7

APPENDIX A

This section provides a brief overview of African Caliphs, exploring their descriptions by both contemporary and later observers. While this project primarily addresses their rule, these portraits, drawn from various accounts, offer valuable insights into how these rulers were perceived by others. Starting at the close of the 6th century, Arab travelers began exploring North Africa and the Maghreb. Their chroniclers, including figures like al-Bakri and al-Idrissi, recorded observations about the customs, behavior, and religiosity of West African rulers. I present here excerpts from various sources to illustrate how African Caliphs were viewed by the outside world, thereby shedding light on their governance. The following sections detail reports from Arabic, European, and African sources.

ARABIC SOURCES

Al-Bakri

Al-Bakri (1014–1094), one of the earliest and most important sources on West African history, never personally traveled to West Africa but relied on informants who had extensive experience in the region. His accounts are crucial for understanding the early Muslim kings of Black Africa, particularly in Western Sudan.

Warjabi

"The inhabitants are Sudan, who were previously, like all the other Sudan, pagans and worshipped dakakir…until Warjabi b. Rabis became their ruler. He embraced Islam, introduced among them Muslim law and compelled them to observe it, thus opening their eyes to the truth. Warjabi died in the year 432/1040-1 and the people of Takrur are Muslims today. From the town of Takrur you go to Silla. This place too consists of two towns situated on both banks of the Nil, and its inhabitants are Muslims who were converted to Islam by Warjabi, may God have mercy upon him" (Levtzion & Hopkins, 2011, p. 77).

Al-Musulmani (King of Malal/Mali)

"Beyond this county lies another called Malal, the king of which is known as al-musulmani. He is thus called because his country became afflicted with drought one year following another; the inhabitants prayed for rain, sacrificing cattle till they had exterminated almost all of them, but the drought and the misery only increased. The king had as his guest a Muslim who used to read the Koran and was acquainted with the Sunna. To this man the king complained of the calamities that assailed him and his people. The man said: 'O King, if you believed in God (who is exalted) and testified that He is One, and testified as to the prophetic mission of Muhammad (God bless him and give him peace) and if you accepted all the religious laws of Islam, I would pray for your deliverance from your plight and that God's mercy would envelop all the people of your country and that your enemies and adversaries might envy you on that account.' Thus he continued to press the king until the latter accepted Islam and became a sincere Muslim. The man made him recite from the Koran some easy passages and taught him religious obligations and practices which no one may be excused from knowing. Then the Muslim made him wait till the eve of the following Friday, when he ordered him to purify himself by a complete ablution, and clothed him in a cotton garment which he had. The two of them came out towards a mound of earth, and there the Muslim stood praying while the king, standing at his right side, imitated him. Thus they prayed for a part of the night, the Muslim reciting invocations and the king saying 'Amen'. The dawn had just started to break when God caused abundant rain to descend upon them. So the king ordered the idols to be broken and expelled the sorcerers from his country. He and his descendants after him as well as his nobles were sincerely attached to Islam, while the common people of his kingdom remained polytheists. Since then their rulers have been given the title of al-musulmani" (Levtzion & Hopkins, 2011, p. 81–82).

King of Kawkaw (Gao)

"When a king ascends the throne he is handed a signet ring, a sword, and a copy of the Koran which, as they assert, were sent to them by the Commander of the Faithful. Their king is a Muslim, for they entrust the kingship only to Muslims" (Levtzion & Hopkins, 2011, p. 87).

Al-Idrissi

Born in Morocco (1100–1165), al-Idrissi was one of the most renowned Arab writers in the Western world. He provided significant information on the Western Sudan, using independent sources to discuss Black Africa, distinguishing him from other chroniclers of the period.

King of Ghana

"This is the greatest of all the towns of the Sudan in respect of area, the most populous, and the surrounding countries and the other countries of al-Maghrib al-Aqsa. Its people are Muslims, and its king, according to what is reported, belongs to the progeny of Salih b. Abd.-Allah b. al-Hassan b. al-Hassan b. 'Ali b. Abi Talib. The khutba is delivered in his own name, though he pays allegiance to the Abbasid caliph. He has a palace on the bank of the Nil, strongly built, and perfectly fortified. His living quarters are decorated with various drawings and paintings, and provided with glass windows. The palace was built in the year 510 of the Hijira...According to what is related about him, he is the most righteous of men" (Levtzion & Hopkins, 2011, p. 110).

Ibn Bhattuta

Ibn Battuta (1304–1369), a prominent Arab travel writer, was one of the first to meet and document Caliphs in West Africa. During his visit to Mali, he interacted with and observed Mansa Sulayman on multiple occasions. I provide one of his several descriptions of Mansa Sulayman here:

> "The sultan comes out of a door in the corner of the palace with his bow in his hand and his quiver between his shoulders. On his head he wears a shashiyya of gold tied with a golden strap. It has extremities like thin knives and is more than a span long. His clothing consists for the most part of a furry red jubba of the European cloth which is called mutanfas... He walks slowly, with great deliberation, and sometimes halts. When he reaches the bambi he stands looking at the people, then he mounts gently, in the same way that the khatib mounts the pulpit" (Levtzion & Hopkins, 2011, p. 291).

Ibn Khaldun

Ibn Khaldun (1332–1406), a notable scholar of the period, also provides valuable insights into the West African Caliphs, particularly in reference to Mansa Musa of the Malian Empire. His works contribute to understanding the characteristics and leadership qualities of these influential Muslim rulers.

> "Mansa Musa was an upright man and a great king, and tales of his justice are still told. He made the Pilgrimage in 724/1324... This man Mansa Musa came from his country with 80 loads of gold dust, each load weighing three qintars...There were

APPENDIX A

diplomatic relations and exchanges of gifts between this sultan Mansa Musa and the contemporary Merinid king of the Maghrib, sultan Abu l-Hasan. High-ranking statesmen of the two kingdoms were exchanged as ambassadors" (Levtzion and Hopkins, 2011, p. 332–5).

EUROPEAN SOURCES

Mungo Park

The European explorer Mungo Park (1771–1806) visited Bundu in the 18th century during the reign of Almaamy Sega Gai (Gomez, 1992). In 1796, Park met Sega Gai under a shade tree, where they conversed while seated on a mat. Park's traveling companions described Sega Gai as a non-Muslim ruler overseeing a predominantly Muslim state. Park, without further inquiry, adopted this assessment. However, both Park and his companions were far from accurate. In reality, Sega Gai came from a long line of Muslim rulers. His reign was marked by internal and external tensions, largely due to his disregard for Islamic law. According to Park, Sega Gai was kind and generous, providing much-needed provisions and taking his role as a gracious host seriously. However, based on the accounts of Park's companions, one can reasonably infer that Sega Gai was losing the faith and respect of those around him. Ultimately, at the end of his reign, Sega Gai was executed in front of his own troops for attacking Muslim towns without provocation and enslaving their inhabitants, actions contrary to Islamic law.

Dr. Heinrich Barth

The German explorer Dr. Heinrich Barth (1821–1865) traveled extensively through several African states during his five-year exploration of the interior of Africa. Notably, he met

Shehu Umar al-Amin, the ruler of Borno. In his diary, Dr. Barth described his encounter: "He found the Sheikh reclining upon a divan in a fine, airy hall. He was of a glossy Black colour, with regular features... dressed in a light tobe, with a bournous wrapped round his shoulder, and a dark red shawl round his head with great care" (Kingston, year, p. 159). This brief description of Shehu Umar offers valuable insight. Shehu Umar was the son of the esteemed Muhammad al-Kanemi al-Amin, an Arab of fair complexion. Despite the physical resemblance to his father, the throne was passed to Shehu Umar, who possessed superior knowledge and leadership abilities. This decision challenges common notions of racial prejudice often ascribed to African societies. Shehu Umar was known for his piety and meticulous attention to detail, qualities essential for governing a highly Islamized society like Borno. Dr. Barth also accompanied Shehu Umar on an excursion to Lake Chad.

Paul Soleillet (1879)

In 1879, the French explorer Paul Soleillet visited Segu, where he sought information on Sheikh al-Hajj Umar Tall. Drawing from various accounts and memories of those present during the Sheikh's conquest of Segu, he constructed a composite picture (Robinson, 1999). Soleillet described the Sheikh as follows: "The Shaikh was always simply clothed: a small calico cap, short turbans, a white shirt and pants covered with a light blue robe, and yellow slippers. In his hand, he carried a small metal pot and, on important occasions, one of his two canes. He was strikingly handsome. His eyes were clear, his skin bronzed, his features symmetrical. His beard was black, long, soft, and divided at the chin. He wore no mustache" (Robinson, 1999, p. 100).

APPENDIX A

Major Dixon Denham (1823)

In 1823, Major Dixon Denham led an expedition to Borno, where he was granted an audience with Sheikh Muhammad al-Amin al-Kanemi, the Caliph of the Borno Empire. Denham described the Caliph as follows:

> "Nature has bestowed on him all the qualifications for a great commander; an enterprising genius, sound judgment, features engaging, with a demeanour gentle and conciliating: and so little of vanity was there mixed with his ambition, that he refused the offer of being made sultan" (Dixon, Denham, & Oudney, 1826, p. 248).

Hugh Clapperton (1824)

Captain Hugh Clapperton was the first European to visit the Sokoto Caliphate in present-day Nigeria during his 1824 expedition (Umar, 2002). He made two journeys to the region, spending significant time with Caliph Muhammad Bello. Clapperton also visited the Borno Empire and met Sheikh Muhammad al-Kanemi, the Empire's Caliph. Regarding the appearance of Muhammad Bello, Clapperton writes:

> "The sultan is a noble-looking man, forty-four years of age, although much younger in appearance, five feet ten inches high, portly in person, with a short curling black beard, a small mouth, a fine forehead, a Grecian nose, and large black eyes. He was dressed in a light blue cotton tobe, with a white muslin turban, the shawl of which he wore over the nose and mouth in the Tuarick fashion" (Denham, 1828, p. 302).

AFRICAN SOURCES

It is important to include descriptions of African Caliphs from West African sources. Although few written records of African Caliphs by their contemporaries survive, many descriptions have been preserved orally and later transcribed by scholars. Below are a few descriptions of African Caliphs from the oral tradition in Hausaland, later recorded in written form.

Muhammadu Kanta, Chief of Kebbi

"According to tradition, Kanta's father came to Hausaland from the east and settled in Katsina. In due course he was appointed head of his village and given the title of Magaji. He married a Hausa woman and she bore him two sons of whom the elder was Kanta. As a boy, Kanta showed exceptional strength and skill in boxing, wrestling, and all the pastimes of youth. As a young man, however, he was headstrong and turbulent and was often in trouble with his elders. When his father died, therefore, he was not chosen to succeed him. The loss of his father's office and title was a severe blow to Kanta's pride and caused him to leave his village and go out into the world to seek his fortune. After leaving Katsina, Kanta went west across Gobir and Zamfara, which were then the most westerly of the Hausa States, and did not stop until he was beyond the Rima. He settled in a remote village called Surame and before long was joined there by a number of former companions and kindred spirits. Now Surame at that time was in the territory of Sarkin Burmi. He found Kanta and his followers so unruly and obstreperous that he determined to teach them a lesson. He therefore led a small party of armed men against them with the idea of bringing them to heel. But instead of submitting, Kanta and his companions turned out to fight. In the skirmish which followed, Sarkin Burmi's henchmen were all killed or overpowered and Sarkin Burmi, it is said, was strangled by Kanta's own hands. After this fight, Kanta's followers hailed him as Sarkin Burmi, using the title of the man he had killed. He rejected it, however, and said: 'It is under my own name that I shall go and the world shall soon learn to recognize the meaning of Kanta.' The valley of the Rima River where Kanta and his followers had established themselves was in the debatable lands between the Hausa States in the east and the Songhai Empire in the west. When Askia the Great marched into Hausaland in the year 1513, Kanta enlisted under him and by the time the

APPENDIX A

campaign was over he had become a man of some importance. Two years after subjugating Hausaland, Askia led his army against the desert State of Air and again Kanta marched with him. This expedition was also successful and Air was annexed to Songhai. When the booty came to be divided, however, Kanta was dissatisfied with the share which he received. This caused him to break with Askia and renounce his allegiance to Gao. Soon afterwards, Askia sent an army against Kanta to crush his rebellion but Kanta defeated it and preserved the independence which he had declared. This victory marked the birth of Kebbi, the last of the Hausa States to come into being. Kanta ruled Kebbi for thirty-five years and raised it from nothing to be the greatest power in Hausaland. He subdued all his neighbours and made them pay tribute to him instead of to Bornu or Songhai as they had before. To the north he conquered Asben and Air, to the south Nupe and Borgu, to the east Zamfara and Zazzau, and to the west Arewa and Zaberma. His dominions extended from the Niger to the Sahara and while he lived he successfully defied the older empires which lay to the east and west of him. In all Kanta built three capitals. To help him build Surame, the last of the three, he exacted men and money from all the states which paid him tribute. It is related that at this time the Tuaregs incurred his displeasure and that he punished them by refusing to let them draw the water which they needed for their work from the Rima. Instead, he made them send their camels many days' journey to the north to fetch water from their own country. Similarly, when the Nupes were late in coming to work, he denied them water and told them that they must send home for shea nut oil and mix their mortar with that. As part of the palace in Surame, Kanta constructed a szratz across a dry moat. If when trying a case he was doubtful whether a man was innocent or guilty he would order him to cross it. Those who crossed successfully were pronounced innocent and set free. Those who did not, fell to the sharpened stakes, red-hot embers, or wild beasts which were waiting below and were deemed to have been guilty. Bornu was the old suzerain of thé Hausa States and with Bornu Kanta was frequently at war. Once a Bornu army marched right across Hausaland and, after defeating the Kebbawa in the field, besieged them in their own capital. The defenders had lost many men in the battle and the Bornu commander thought that final victory was within his grasp. When his men marched up to the walls for the final assault, however, they were dismayed to find every embrasure manned. Many of the defenders were in fact dead men propped up in their places, but Kanta had caused their lips to be slit so that they seemed to be grinning down at the enemy. Their stares so unnerved the Bornu commander that he called off the assault, raised the siege, and marched his army away. This event has been commemorated in the phrase 'dariya ba loto' or 'laughter without end'" (Johnston, 1966, 116–119).

Sarkin Kano Muhammadu Rumfa (1463–1499)

"The twentieth Chief of Kano was Muhammadu dan Yakubu, known as Muhammadu Rumfa, whose mother came from Rano and was called Fadimatu. He was an upright man, a righteous man, and a learned man. Kano has never had, nor ever will have, another Chief to equal him. It was in his time that the Sherifs first came to Kano, Abdur Rahman and his followers. Of Abdur Rahman it is related that the Prophet came to him in a dream and said: 'Arise and go to the west and strengthen Islam there.' On setting out he took some of the dust of Medina and put it in his bag and brought it with him to Hausaland. At every town he came to, he took a little dust and mixed it with the dust of Medina and when he saw that they did not match he passed on. He continued to do this until he came to Kano, but when he took the dust of Kano and mixed it with the dust of Medina it became as one. Whereupon he said: "This is the town which I saw in my dream.' So he lodged at Panisau and sent a message to the Chief in the city. And the Chief came out to him and escorted him back to the city and with him were his companions Hantari and Gemindodo and Gadangemi and Alfagi and others to the number of ten. So Abdur Rahman stopped in Kano and strengthened Islam. He had brought many books with him and he gave Rumfa religious instruction. He built the mosque in the city. He cut down the juju tree and erected a minaret in its

APPENDIX A

place. By the time he had done, the city was full of Mallams and the state was united in Islam. Leaving Sidi Fari behind him, he therefore returned to Egypt. Sarkin Kano Rumfa became the originator of twelve things in Kano. First of all he built the palace which is now known as Rumfa's Palace. In the following year he extended the walls of the city from the Dagachi Gate to the Mata Gate to the Gyartawasa Gate to the Kawaye Gate to the Na'isa Gate and thence to the Kansakali Gate. In the year after that, having taken up residence in the Palace, he founded the Kurmi Market and in the war against Katsina it was he who first had spare chargers brought into battle. He was also the first to seize the women of the pagans as concubines, sending Darman into the slave settlements with orders to bring him every virgin whom he found there. He was the first to have a thousand women in his harem and it was he who introduced purdah. It was he, too, who first established the Council of Nine and brought in the long horn and ostrich-feather fans and ostrich-feather slippers. Moreover he was the first to use the Shadokoko prayer-ground for the Moslem festivals and to give titles to eunuchs... . As a Chief, Rumfa had no equal and that is why the epithet 'Paragon among Princes, Cleanser of the State' was coined for him. In his time there was war with Katsina. The fighting went on for eleven years but neither side prevailed. In all Rumfa reigned for thirty-seven years" (Palmer, 1908, p. 77–8).

The list of descriptions is not exhaustive, as many other explorers, merchants, traders, and soldiers visited African Caliphs during Africa's Classical Islamic period. They interacted with Islamic rulers, and additional African sources describe Caliphs in various roles. However, the portraits provided above offer valuable insights into both the personalities and governance of African Caliphs. From these early accounts, we observe that they were not only warriors and Islamic scholars but also administrators who managed vast territories, commerce, and diverse populations. These Caliphs were central to interstate commerce, connecting the resource-rich African continent with the rest of the world. Aware of their value, they defended their wealth with great ferocity.

These descriptions also highlight an important distinction between the rulers of Muslim West Africa and their counterparts elsewhere. Specifically, the depictions demonstrate the simplicity of dress and regalia among West African Muslim rulers. Even the most learned Caliphs, such as Muhammad Bello and Muhammad al-Kanemi (of the Sokoto Caliphate and the Borno-Kanem Empire, respectively), typically avoided pomp, instead embodying simplicity and piety in their appearance and behavior. This contrasts sharply with the elaborate regalia often worn by princes in Europe, India, and China during the same period. Notably, there are exceptions, particularly with the Caliphs of the Malian and Songhay empires. Mansa Musa, for instance, was renowned for the gold his entourage carried. Similarly, as ruler of the Songhay Empire, Askia Dawud would have up to 700 eunuchs present during royal audiences (Gomez, 2018, p. 307). These displays of wealth and power, prominent in the 14th and 15th centuries, became less common in later years. Modesty, self-discipline, and piety increasingly became markers of a ruler's significance, especially after the Muslim revolutions in West Africa during the 17th and 18th centuries.

REFERENCES

Denham, D. (1828). *Narrative of travels and discoveries in Northern and Central Africa, in the years 1822, 1823, and 1824* (Vol. II). John Murray.

Denham, D., Clapperton, H., & Oudney, W. (1826). *Narrative of travels and discoveries in Northern and Central Africa, in the years 1822, 1823, and 1824*. John Murray.

Gomez, M. (1992). *Pragmatism in the age of jihad: The precolonial state of Bundu*. Cambridge University Press.

APPENDIX A

Gomez, M. (2018). *African dominion: A new history of empire in early and medieval West Africa*. Princeton University Press.

Johnston, H. A. S. (1966). *A selection of Hausa stories*. Clarendon Press.

Levtzion, N., & Hopkins, J. F. P. (2011). *Corpus of early Arabic sources for West African history*. Markus Wiener Publishers.

Palmer, H. R. (1908). The Kano chronicle. *The Journal of the Royal Anthropological Institute of Great Britain and Ireland, 38*, 58–98.

Robinson, D. (1985). *The holy war of Umar Tal: The Western Sudan in the mid-nineteenth century*. Clarendon Press.

Umar, M. S. (2002). Islamic discourses on European visitors to Sokoto Caliphate in the nineteenth century. *Studia Islamica, 95*, 135–159.

AFTERWARDS

The political heritage of Africa offers insights that can enrich modern thought, much as the European political heritage has. However, what are the main sources of Africa's political heritage? In the Western context, the sources of political leadership are widely recognized. Scholars agree that the foundations of Western political leadership trace back to ancient Greece and Rome. For example, the American political tradition is deeply rooted in classical Greek and Roman political theory and practices. This legacy is reflected in foundational documents like the Federalist Papers and the U.S. Constitution, as well as in political institutions such as the federal, executive, and legislative branches.

But what about the sources of political leadership for Americans of non-European backgrounds? Some groups, such as Chinese Americans, are well aware of their political heritage, with a long history of Chinese political leadership. Similarly, Persian Americans, Arab Americans, Mexican Americans, and Irish Americans can trace their political legacies with clarity.

However, many African Americans have not had the same advantage. Unlike other groups who often look to their ancestral homelands for political guidance, African Americans faced a historical erasure of their heritage during slavery, and their ancestral history was frequently downplayed in formal education (Woodson, 1990). As a result, African Americans have historically been at a disadvantage in leveraging their rich political traditions to address contemporary social challenges.

THE AFRICAN CALIPHS

When discussing African American leadership heritage, scholars rarely bridge the gap between African and American experiences. Many argue that African Americans are a "brand new" people, but this view overlooks extensive research that demonstrates otherwise. African Americans, like any other group, retain significant aspects of their ancestral culture, language, and political traditions. Those who assert that African Americans are a "brand new" people should consider the work of scholars like Melville Herskovits (1941) and Lorenzo Dow Turner (1949), whose research highlights the deep social and cultural connections between Africa and African Americans. Herskovits (1941) in particular provides compelling evidence debunking the myth that African Americans lack a connection to their African heritage, culture, and language. These connections persist today, and analyzing the political behavior of precolonial African leaders offers valuable insights into contemporary African American politics.

In their analysis of African American leadership, Walters and Smith (1999) begin their survey in the 1930s, overlooking the period of American slavery. While they have valid reasons for this choice, their approach excludes key elements of leadership during slavery and its connections to leadership traditions in both Africa and America. Historical records highlight the significant role of enslaved African Muslims in providing leadership within American slave societies. For example, Bilali Muhammad, a slave in Georgia, was originally an Almaamy (Muslim political leader) from Futa Jallon (modern-day Guinea). According to Austin (2012), Bilali continued to provide leadership during his captivity in America. Diouf (2013) recounts how, during the American War of 1812, Bilali refused to defect to the British, who had promised freedom to slaves who joined their ranks, and he declared, "he wouldn't defect to the British – who had promised freedom to the slaves if they joined their ranks – and could answer for every Negro of the true faith" (Diouf, 2013, p. 125). Bilali Muhammad and his neighbor, Salih Bilali, wielded considerable political influence over more than 80 slaves in the area. This incident underscores the respect both Black and White communities had for Bilali and his reputation. Bilali also saved many lives during a major natural disaster, demonstrating his responsibility to others, even while enslaved. Such local Black leaders during America's antebellum years are often overlooked in favor of national figures. Bilali Muhammad's leadership challenges in Africa and America demonstrate the complexity of his political role in both contexts.

Another notable political leader from this period is Abdul Rahman Ibrahima Sori. Sori was the son of the Almaamy in Futa Jallon before being captured and enslaved in the American South (Alford, 2007). He gained his freedom through a fortuitous encounter. A White doctor, who had fallen ill while visiting the coast of Guinea, was sent to the Almaamy (Sori's father) for treatment. The doctor was nursed back to health under the Almaamy's care. Years later, while in Natchez, Mississippi, the doctor encountered Sori and recognized him as the son of the man who had saved his life in Africa. The doctor then worked to secure Sori's freedom.

Upon his release, Sori traveled across the United States, delivering speeches and lectures on various significant issues. He met with key officials in Washington, D.C., and corresponded directly with American diplomats. His literary talents, particularly his ability to read and write Arabic, his memorization of the Qur'an, and his dignified deportment as a distinguished gentleman, captivated audiences, especially considering his 40 years of enslavement. Sori also visited African American churches, lodges, and other Black venues, using his platform to address political issues and share his experiences. He spoke about the horrors of slavery and compared the lives of Blacks in America to those in Africa, expressing a preference for life in Africa. Additionally, Sori became one of the first public promoters of Islam in America, particularly among African Americans. He believed that both Americans and African Americans could greatly benefit from the Islamic faith (Alford, 2007).

This period predated the 19th century, illustrating the deep historical connections between Black leadership in America and Africa. Instances like this appear throughout the record of American slavery. While African leaders were often brought to America as captives, many continued to exert political influence in various forms. These connections persisted beyond slavery, as a branch of the Royal House of Sori (direct descendants of Abdul Rahman Ibrahima Sori) remains in Natchez, Mississippi, to this day. Many of these descendants provide local leadership and maintain cultural and political exchanges with relatives in West Africa.

Despite efforts to erase the African heritage of African Americans and other Diasporan Africans, significant works have uncovered the African past and its connections to contemporary political realities (Gomez, 2019; Sudarkasa, 1986; Association of Black Women Historians et al., 1989). Since Carter G. Woodson's seminal work (1939|2016), scholars have highlighted the contributions of African civilizations to the broader human experience. One major assumption underlying this body of work is that Africa, the second most populous continent, offers valuable insights into political leadership. I examine political leadership in Africa to enhance our collective understanding of political dynamics. The political legacy of African leaders can provide contemporary observers with a richer understanding and appreciation of both the science and art of political leadership.

AFTERWARDS

I conclude this section with a brief account of a significant event in the 19th-century Caliphate of Sudan. During this period, the visionary religious leader Muhammad Ahmad declared himself the Mahdi (the expected one from Allah) and initiated a religious revolution aimed at achieving Sudan's independence and ending centuries of colonial oppression. In his campaign, he successfully defeated three colonial powers: Egypt, Turkey, and Great Britain. Notably, Muhammad Ahmad is the only Caliph to have both defended his territory from colonial forces and expanded it without ever suffering a defeat.

After Ahmad's death from natural causes, a *shura* (religious consultative meeting) was convened to determine his successor as Caliph. A tense debate ensued, with many participants vocally advocating for their preferred candidate. The family of Muhammad Ahmad believed that the successor should come from within its own ranks. Throughout this contentious process, Abdullahi, Muhammad Ahmad's second-in-command, remained silent. Eventually, it was decided that Abdullahi should assume the title of Caliph, owing to his regal bearing and demonstration of the qualities necessary to uphold the prestige of the throne. His demeanor during the debate was the most Caliph-like. Abdullahi was the only one who did not debase himself by actively seeking the mantle of representing Allah's Holy Messenger on earth. Thus, in Sudan, Abdullahi assumed the title of Khalifa Abdullahi.

This episode illustrates that one's fitness for leadership should not be contingent upon the position becoming available. Rather, one should live in a manner that inspires confidence and respect. This principle was one of the reasons Muhammad Ahmad chose Khalifa Abdullahi as his main representative, even over his own brothers and other relatives.

Although this event took place in East Africa, it also had implications for West Africa. When Muhammad Ahmad declared himself the Mahdi, influential figures from West African Caliphates, such as Borno and Sokoto, traveled to Sudan to join the Mahdist forces. Several West African leaders, concerned about the growing number of Ahmad's supporters, attempted to prevent their citizens from joining the movement.

This succession episode exemplifies the type of leadership admired across various African Islamic polities. It also offers a parallel to American political leadership. For instance, George Washington, the first president of the United States, was unanimously elected by his peers, despite never campaigning for office or soliciting votes. In contrast, contemporary political candidates who display such humility and grace would likely not make it past the initial stages of a campaign. This narrative is significant because it highlights the shared leadership values of humility, grace, and the ability to inspire confidence and respect, which were once admired in American political circles. This comparison emphasizes the timeless and cross-cultural nature of effective leadership qualities and suggests that contemporary political discourse could benefit from examining the leadership examples of the African past.

REFERENCES

Alford, T. (2007). *Prince among slaves: The true story of an African prince sold into slavery in the American South* (30th anniversary ed.). Oxford University Press.

Association of Black Women Historians, Terborg-Penn, R., Harley, S., & Rushing, A. B. (1989). *Women in Africa and the African diaspora*. Howard University Press.

Asante, M. K. (2000). *The Egyptian philosophers: Ancient African voices from Imhotep to Akhenaten*. Menaibuc.

Austin, A. (2012). *African Muslims in antebellum America: Transatlantic stories and spiritual struggles*. Routledge.

Diouf, S. A. (2013). Servants of Allah: African Muslims Enslaved in the Americas. In *Servants of Allah*. New York University Press.

AFTERWARDS

Gomez, M. (2019). *Reversing sail: A history of the African diaspora.* Cambridge University Press.

Hamilton, A., Madison, J., & Jay, J. (2005). *The Federalist papers.* Signet Classics.

Herskovits, M. J. (1941). *The myth of the negro past.* Harpers.

Martin, G. (2012). *African political thought.* Palgrave Macmillan.

Sudarkasa, N. (1986). The status of women in indigenous African societies. *Feminist Studies, 12*(1), 91–103.

Turner, L. (1949). *Africanisms in the Gullah dialect.* University of Chicago Press.

Woodson, C. G. (1939|2016). *African heroes and heroines* (Reprint ed., The Woodson Series). Black Classic Press.

Woodson, C. G. (1990). *The mis-education of the Negro.* Africa World Press.

www.ingramcontent.com/pod-product-compliance
Lightning Source LLC
Chambersburg PA
CBHW020544030426
42337CB00013B/969